Handbook
of
Speech Improvement

CHARLES KENNETH THOMAS

PROFESSOR OF SPEECH AND
DIRECTOR OF THE SPEECH CLINIC
CORNELL UNIVERSITY

THE RONALD PRESS COMPANY · NEW YORK

PREFACE

This book is one result of more than thirty years' experience in helping students to improve their speech. It is designed for those people whose speech lacks accuracy or distinctness, fails to give the impression of a good social background, or suggests the patterns of another language. It does not deal with problems of voice, with such organic difficulties as cleft palate or cerebral palsy, nor with the functional difficulties of stuttering. Those difficulties require different treatment from the difficulties considered in this book.

Language consists of a system of vocal signals. For the system to operate, the signals must be kept distinct. On the theoretical level, this requirement leads to the phonemic principle. On the practical level, in this book, it means that a large number of the exercises provide opportunities for contrasting one sound with others. These contrasts should be well under control before the student practices other exercises for uniformity of sound. The book, however, is not prescriptive in setting up one standard of American pronunciation.

Since English spelling is notoriously unreliable as a guide to English sounds, the sounds are identified throughout the book by the symbols of the International Phonetic Association, in the form most commonly used in the United States. These are the same symbols as those in my earlier book, *An Introduction to the Phonetics of American English* (New York: The Ronald Press Company, 1947), to which the student may refer for a more complete discussion of the sounds.

Many people have contributed, directly or indirectly, to this book. Over the years I have learned from colleagues and from those students whose special difficulties have stimulated me to develop better methods for coping with them. In the actual writing I owe a special debt of gratitude to Robert W. Albright and Mrs. Joy B. Albright, and to members of my family: Ruth, Arthur, and Andrew Thomas. These five people have examined the manuscript and have challenged everything they could find to challenge. They have made many helpful suggestions. Final responsibility for the contents of the book must, of course, rest with me alone.

C. K. THOMAS

Ithaca, New York
January, 1956

CONTENTS

PAGE

PART I. INTRODUCTION 1

PART II. CONSONANTS 15

    LIP CONSONANTS 15

    LIP-TEETH CONSONANTS 22

    LIP-BACK CONSONANTS 28

    TONGUE-TEETH CONSONANTS . . . 32

    GUM-RIDGE CONSONANTS 40

    THE CONSONANT [r] 54

    HARD-PALATE CONSONANTS 60

    SOFT-PALATE CONSONANTS 80

    THE CONSONANT [h] 96

PART III. VOWELS AND DIPHTHONGS . . 99

    FRONT VOWELS 101

    BACK VOWELS 108

    CENTRAL VOWELS WITH [r] 122

    DIPHTHONGS 126

INDEX OF SOUNDS 133

HANDBOOK OF
SPEECH IMPROVEMENT

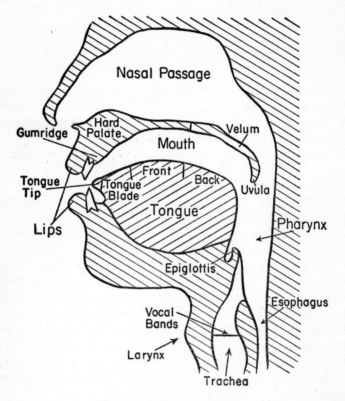

Diagram of Speech Mechanism

Part I

INTRODUCTION

We are so accustomed to language, we use it for so many hours
a day, that we usually lose sight of its basic nature. Essentially
it is a system of signals that enables its users to exchange in-
formation, opinions, and attitudes, and to get the daily work done
coöperatively. Because language is so complicated, we usually
overlook its relationship to simpler systems of signaling.

We wave a wordless greeting to a friend. We whistle for the
dog. The traffic cop stops us at the corner with his upraised
palm. Though all these are signals, we do not ordinarily stop to
give them the label. Perhaps the simplest set of signals that we
recognize as signals is the familiar three-way code of traffic lights.

All motorists know that green means go and red means stop,
even when they ignore the meaning. Not all agree on the exact
meaning of the amber light, but in general it indicates some need
for caution. For the system to work, the signals must be understood. They are arbitrary, and the motorist must learn the code.
A Rip Van Winkle descending from the hills after a longer sleep
than Washington Irving's original would interpret the flashing
red and green traffic lights no differently from the flashing neon
signs used to emphasize advertisements.

But the signals need not be absolutely uniform. Some red
traffic lights have more orange in them than others, some greens
more yellow or blue. It matters only that the signals be enough
different from one another to leave no doubt as to their meaning.
In a complicated system of signals like a language, the principles
already indicated must be kept in mind. Just as Rip Van Winkle
must learn the traffic-light code, so the child must learn the code
of his native language, and the foreigner in America learns that
the code of English is different from that of his native language.

On the other hand, just as traffic-light green may shade toward yellow or blue, similar minor variations occur in the linguistic code. No two of us pronounce the word *cat* with exactly the same shade of vowel. A general sense of green serves for the traffic light, and a general awareness of the vowel in *cat* being different from that of *cot* or *kettle* prevents linguistic traffic accidents.

Of the virtually unlimited variety of utterances which the human vocal cords, tongue, lips, jaw, and oral and nasal chambers can produce, most languages use about forty meaningfully different signals. In contrast to the simple three-way traffic code, we must be able to make about forty recognizably different sounds in English, the exact number depending on the type of English used. We make slight variations in our pronunciation of *cat*, but must not let those variations reach the point of sounding like *cot*. We must not confuse *cattle* with *kettle*, or *bill* with *pill*.

Two technical terms will be useful at this point: the phoneme and the allophone. The phoneme is the signaling unit. It is what distinguishes *cat* from *cot*, from *hat*, and from *cap*. We say that *cat* contains three phonemes because we can change the meaning by substituting other phonemes for each of the three successive sounds. The phoneme is, in a sense, an abstraction. It corresponds to traffic-light green. But as we have seen, neither traffic-light green nor the pronunciation of *cat* is absolutely uniform, and the variations in the actual pronunciation of the vowel in *cat* are the allophones of that particular vowel phoneme. The allophones represent the phoneme, and constitute the variations which do not produce ambiguity.

The phonemic systems of different languages do not necessarily correspond with one another. Both Spanish and Japanese use a similar but not identical five-vowel system. The [u]* of Japanese *Fujiyama* is by no means the same as the [u] of Spanish *mucho,* nor are either of them the same as the [u] of English *food.* All three languages set up different groupings of pho-

---

* Here as elsewhere throughout the book, letters in square brackets are phonetic symbols which refer to sounds, usually to phonemes, occasionally to important allophones. Letters in *italics* refer to spellings. Thus we can say that the word *honor* contains an *h,* but no [h].

nemes, and cluster different sets of allophones around the phonemes. Since English vowel phonemes are more numerous than
either Spanish or Japanese, the range of English allophonic variation is correspondingly restricted.

English makes a phonemic contrast between *gate* and *get*. No
such contrast is possible in Spanish. English contrasts *sin, shin,*
chin, and *gin,* but the phonemic system of Tagalog, and of other
Philippine languages, makes such contrast impossible. Italian
uses all four of these consonantal contrasts, but French only those
of *sin* and *shin,* Spanish only those of *sin* and *chin.* English distinguishes between *seat* and *sit*; no such contrast is possible in
Italian. German distinguishes between *Bruder* and *Brüder.* No
such contrast is possible in English; if a similar variation in sound
occurs in English it is merely an accidental, allophonic variation.
In short, when you start to learn a new language, you have to
know what the phonemes are, and what variations in the allophones can be used without ambiguity. The pattern of phonemes
and allophones is different in each language.

The phonemic patterns sometimes change at different his-
torical stages of the language. No longer do *food, good,* and
blood constitute the exact rhymes they did at the end of the six-
teenth century; no longer are *sea* and *say* identical in sound, as
they were at the beginning of the eighteenth.

Even within the limits of a single language at a single time,
the phonemic patterns may be somewhat different. In an American Indian language spoken by a few hundred members of a
single tribe, there may be relative uniformity. In a world-wide
language, like Spanish or English, there are bound to be differences. Madrid and Buenos Aires do not begin *cinco,* the numeral
five, with the same consonant phoneme; Madrid has an extra
phoneme [θ], like the initial English phoneme in *think,* which
Buenos Aires lacks. In eastern New England, *balm* and *bomb*
are regularly distinguished by different vowel phonemes. In
much of the rest of the United States and Canada they are pronounced with identical phonemes, and differentiated only by
context.

Thus, although every speaker speaks differently from other
speakers in some details, nevertheless we recognize that in large

communities most people speak enough alike for the differences to pass unnoticed. And in larger areas people speak enough alike to avoid serious hindering of communication. In Portland, Maine, people go about their business and communicate with each other without noticing anything unusual. To the visiting Philadelphian, however, the Portlanders will sound different, but understandable. The same situation holds true, in reverse, if the Portlander visits Philadelphia. Portland, Philadelphia, Savannah, Tulsa, and Seattle have more in common than not, and it is with this large area of common speech that this book is largely concerned.

There is good speech anywhere in the English-speaking world, and there is bad speech. You do not improve bad Tulsa speech by adding a watered-down flavor of Boston. Nor do you improve bad Boston speech by adding a watered-down flavor of London or Chicago. You aim for the best speech of the area in which you do your work and have your contacts. And if you acquire good speech there, you won't have much to do to adapt yourself to another area. You won't necessarily have to do any adapting at all, since good Philadelphia speech will be acceptable in Portland, and good Chicago speech in New York, to all but the most provincial.

But to improve your speech you must know what speech is, and you must know it in detail. A system of spelling that represents a single vowel sound by means of the variety of spellings illustrated in *be, bee, sea, machine, Cæsar, people, receive,* and *believe* will not be much help in analysis of the sounds. Neither will a system that uses the letter *a* to represent the quite different vowel sounds in *at, ate, arm, any, all,* and *about.* For analysis of the phonemes we need a set of symbols, arbitrarily chosen, in which each symbol represents a single English phoneme, and in which each English phoneme is always represented by that symbol. Those symbols, as already noted, will be enclosed in square brackets to avoid confusion with symbols used to indicate spelling, which will be italicized. We also need to know something about the ways in which the sounds are formed, their relationships to one another, and the places they may occupy in the stream of connected speech.

Consonants

All English speech is produced by outgoing breath, but six consonants constitute a group in which the outgoing breath stream is momentarily interrupted. We call these sounds stops because of the momentary stoppage of the breath. The six are [p] as in *pill*, [t] as in *till*, [k] as in *kill*, [b] as in *bill*, [d] as in *dill*, and [g] as in *gill* or *give*. Of these, [p], [t], and [k] are voiceless; the outgoing breath stream is not accompanied by any vibration of the vocal cords in the throat. The other three, [b], [d], and [g], are voiced; the outgoing breath passes through the vibrating vocal cords, which impart a musical tone to the consonants. The voiceless sounds are produced more energetically that the voiced. For [p] and [b], the interruption of the breath stream is brought about by pressing both lips together. For [t] and [d] the tip of the tongue touches the upper gums. For [k] and [g], the back of the tongue presses against the soft palate. For all six, the soft-palate valve must be closed to prevent diversion of the breath stream into the nose. Examples:

[p]   as in *pill*, *upper*, and *cup*.
[t]   as in *till*, *utter*, and *cut*.
[k]   as in *kill*, *anchor*, *car*, and *quick*.
[b]   as in *bill*, *rubber*, and *rob*.
[d]   as in *dill*, *rudder*, and *rod*.
[g]   as in *gill*, *soggy*, and *sag*.

Three nasal sounds share the places of articulation utilized by the stops: [m] in *sum*, [n] in *sun*, and [ŋ] in *sung*. For [m] we close the lips, as for [p] and [b]. For [n] we place the tip of the tongue on the gum ridge, as for [t] and [d]. For [ŋ] we place the back of the tongue on the soft palate, as for [k] and [g]. For all three, however, the soft-palate valve remains open, so that the breath stream is not stopped, but diverted through the nose. All three are voiced; voiceless allophones do not change the meaning. Of the three, [ŋ] is limited in the positions it may occupy in the English pattern. It may be used only after certain vowel sounds: those of *string, strength, rang, gong, wrong,* or *hung.* It may not be used at the beginning of a word or syllable, nor before final [g]. In the middle of words it may occur before [g], as in *single,* or before other sounds, as in *singer.* Examples:

> [m] as in *may, summer,* and *aim.*
> [n] as in *no, sinner,* and *own.*
> [ŋ] as in *sing, singer, single,* and *ink.*

Four pairs of consonants take their characteristic sound quality from the friction of the breath being forced through a narrow opening. These consonants require more breath pressure than the nasals, but less than the stops. [f] narrows the passageway by placing the lower lip against the upper teeth. It is voiceless; the corresponding voiced sound, made with the same adjustment of lip and teeth, is [v]. [θ] narrows the passageway by placing the tip of the tongue against or between the teeth. It is voiceless; the corresponding voiced sound is [ð]. [s] narrows the passageway by raising some part of the tongue close to the upper gum ridge and by developing a narrow groove down the midline of the tongue. It is voiceless; the corresponding voiced sound is [z]. [ʃ] arches the tongue slightly further back, and without the midline groove. It is voiceless; the corresponding voiced sound is [ʒ]. Peculiarities of English spelling show vividly in this set of sounds. The letter *s* may represent [s], [z], [ʃ], or [ʒ]. The letter *z* may represent [z], [s], or [ʒ]. Except for a limited number of people who use [ʒ] at the end of a few words like *rouge,* [ʒ] occurs only in the middle of English words. Examples:

> [f] as in *fall, off, cough, philosophy.*
> [v] as in *veal, of, even.*
> [θ] as in *thin, ether, path.*
> [ð] as in *this, either, smooth.*
> [s] as in *see, ace, passing, waltz.*
> [z] as in *zone, buzzard, rose.*
> [ʃ] as in *she, sure, passion, nation, ocean, machine, fish.*
> [ʒ] as in *measure, azure,* and sometimes *rouge.*

Two other sounds include frictional elements, both voiceless. [h] develops some friction as the breath passes through the voice box, or larynx, but has no fixed mouth position. [ʍ] involves friction at the lips, which are rounded, and in the back of the mouth, where the tongue is raised toward the soft palate. Both [h] and [ʍ] occur only in initial and medial positions, and many speakers substitute [w] as in *wear* for [ʍ] as in *where*. Examples:

[h] as in *he, who, ahead.*
[ʍ] as in *where, somewhat.*

Two closely blended combinations of stop and fricative may be represented by [tʃ] and [dʒ]. Examples:

[tʃ] as in *cheap, nature, peach.*
[dʒ] as in *joy, age, bridge, soldier.*

The remaining consonants can be grouped in a loose classification known as semivowels. All are voiced. None involve stoppage or audible friction of the breath. In general quality they sound more like the nasals, or like vowels, than any of the previous groupings.

[l] is a lateral semivowel formed by placing the tip of the tongue on the gum ridge and allowing the breath to escape around one or both sides. Examples: *lull* and *valley.*

[r] is formed by raising either the tip or the central part of the tongue. It occurs initially, medially, and finally for most Americans, but some use it only before an immediately following vowel. Examples: *red, berry, far,* and *farm.* Those who restrict its use to the position immediately before a vowel do not use it in *far* and *farm,* but compensate for its loss by prolonging the vowel. What was once a consonantal [r] in *firm, turn, berth,* and *work* is now a vowel [ɝ] or [ɜ].

[j] is formed by raising the front of the tongue toward the hard palate, and using this position as a springboard to the position of a following vowel. Unlike [l] and [r], it is characterized by movement rather than position. Examples: *youth, unit, onion, beauty.*

[w] is formed by rounding the lips, raising the back of the tongue, and using this position as a springboard to the position

of the following vowel. Unlike [l] and [r], but like [j], it is characterized by movement rather than by position. Examples: *west, quite, choir.*

English Vowels

We differentiate English vowels by height of tongue, region of tongue, muscular tension, and, to a lesser degree, by lip rounding. The tongue position for vowels may be high, mid-high, or low. The raised portion of the tongue may be front, central, or back. The muscles may be tense or lax.

Examples:

[i] high, front, tense: *eat, bee, receive, believe, machine*
[ɪ] high, front, lax: *it, myth, beer, clear, busy, pretty*
[e] mid, front, tense: *aim, may, great, take*
[ɛ] mid, front, lax: *set, said, fare, many, bury*
[æ] low, front, lax: *sat, plaid*
[ɑ] low, back, lax: *are, hearth, hot*
[ɔ] low, back, tense: *all, north, caught, bought*
[o] mid, back, tense: *go, oak, hoe, blow, bureau*
[ʌ] mid, back, lax: *up, come, flood, rough*
[ʊ] high, back, lax: *put, wolf, shook, could*
[u] high, back, tense: *rude, do, soup, school, shoe*

Of the foregoing, [u] normally has close lip rounding, [o] somewhat less, [ʊ] still less, [ɔ] least of all. Though lip rounding is not essential to the identification of these phonemes, vigorous, though not exaggerated, lip rounding helps distinctness.

The central vowels, those produced by raising the central part of the tongue, require fuller explanation:

[ɝ] is an [r]-colored vowel, mid, central, and tense, which is used only in stressed syllables by those speakers who are said to pronounce their *r*'s. Examples: *berth, earth, birth, worth, turn,* and the stressed syllables of *myrtle, further, working, firmness.*

[ɜ] is a mid, central, tense vowel used in the same words as [ɝ], but by speakers who are said not to pronounce their *r*'s. [ɜ] may be classified as the phoneme corresponding to [ɝ] in those forms of American English which consistently avoid [ɝ]. In mixed speech, [ɝ] and [ɜ] are separate allophones of the same phoneme.

[ɚ] is an [r]-colored mid, central, lax vowel used only in unstressed syllables by those people who are said to pronounce their *r*'s. Examples: *beggar, paper, tapir, actor, murmur,* and *martyr*.

[ə] is a mid, central, lax vowel used only in unstressed positions. It has three sets of uses: (1) as a replacement for [ɚ] in the speech of those people who are said not to pronounce their *r*'s, in *beggar,* etc.; (2) as a replacement for [r] by the same speakers, as in *here, there,* and *poor,* sometimes in *corn* and *door,* and for either [ɚ] or [r] in *hire* and *flour*; (3) as a general unstressed vowel in *soda, taken, April, bacon, circus,* and *gracious.* This last use is extremely important. Some languages do not use reduced vowel quality in unstressed positions, but [ə] is highly characteristic of English. It should not be avoided under the mistaken notion that its avoidance makes English more distinct. To say [sodɑ] instead of [sodə] for *soda,* or [tekɛn] instead of [tekən] for *taken,* is to produce not distinctness but distraction. Do not be afraid to use [ə].

Two other vowels occur in some types of English. Most of you will not need to add them to your supply of vowels, but you should know something about them. The first, [a], is intermediate in sound between the [æ] of *ax* and the [ɑ] of *ox*. It is used by some speakers in eastern New England in such words as *ask, dance,* and *path,* in which most Americans use [æ]; and in such words as *arm, calm,* and *father,* in which most Americans use [ɑ]. Some speakers in eastern Virginia use [a] in words like *ask, dance,* and *path,* but not in words like *arm, calm,* and *father.* In the Great Lakes area, stretching from western New England to the central Dakotas, some speakers use [a] in words like *hot, stop, lock,* and *on.* Native speakers of Spanish usually approximate [a] for the Spanish *a.* In learning English they might better discard [a] and concentrate on making the distinction between [æ] and [ɑ]. Native speakers of English who use [a] should feel under no pressure to abandon it, but those who do not use it should feel under no pressure to acquire it.

The second vowel, [ɒ], is intermediate in sound between [ɑ] and [ɔ]. It is used occasionally as a substitute for [ɑ] in such words as *stop, hot,* and *lock*; more frequently as a substitute for [ɔ] in such words as *bought* and *talk*; still more frequently in words like *forest, log,* and *on,* in which the normal variation ranges all the way from [ɑ] to [ɔ]. Unless the use of [ɒ] produces ambiguity, as it does in scattered sections of the United States and Canada, between such pairs of words as *cot* and *caught,* or *nod* and *gnawed,* its use creates no special problems for the native speaker of English.

For the foreigner, however, the aim should be a clear distinction between [ɑ] and [ɔ]. He should avoid [ɒ], especially in such words as *stop, hot,* and *lock,* in which the habits of his native language may encourage him to use the vowel. He will be more readily understandable, in English, if he uses [ɑ] in words of this type. Similarly, he will do well to avoid [a], which he can all too easily substitute for both [æ] and [ɑ]. A clear distinction of the series [æ]-[ɑ]-[ɔ], as in *cat-cot-caught* should be his aim.

Diphthongs

A diphthong is a continuous gliding sound within the limits of a single syllable. To indicate an approximation of the glide we use two vowel symbols which represent the approximate points at which the glide begins and ends. English has three phonemic diphthongs:

[aɪ] as in *ice, fly, aisle,* and *height.*
[ɔɪ] as in *oil, boy, noise,* and *oyster.*
[aʊ] as in *out, now, house,* and *town.*

These diphthongs are phonemic in the sense that they contrast with one another: *buy* [baɪ], *boy* [bɔɪ], and *bough* [baʊ]. They are also phonemic in that they contrast with simple vowel phonemes. Thus *life* [laɪf] contrasts with [laf], which will be interpreted as *laugh* everywhere except in the South. *Boil* [bɔɪl] contrasts with *ball* [bɔl]; *pound* [paʊnd] contrasts with *pond* [pɑnd]. These diphthongs have allophonic variations which will be discussed in full in the sections dealing with the diphthong exercises.

In addition to the phonemic diphthongs, the vowels [i], [e], [o], and [u] often develop gliding allophones. *Seat* may be [sit] or [sɪit]. *Gate* may be [get] or [geɪt]. *Boat* may be [bot] or [boʊt]. *Boot* may be [but] or [bʊut]. Since neither [ɪi], [eɪ], [oʊ], nor [ʊu] affect the meaning, they may properly be regarded as allophones of the vowels [i], [e], [o], and [u]. They are, none the less, stylistically important allophones, and the foreigner, in particular, should learn to use them. They will be discussed in full in the exercises dealing with vowels.

For speech to be understandable we must be able to differentiate between the phonemes described in this chapter. The child born into an English-speaking environment spends several years learning to do just this. He must learn to hear the distinctions and recognize the phonemes as contrasting signals. Then he must learn to produce the allophones that will be recognized as representing the proper phonemes. Until he learns to do this he will be misunderstood. With good intelligence, good hearing, and good models he will be motivated to recognize and produce the necessary sounds. Only then can he make his wants known.

Unfortunately, not all children make such progress. Many grow up with indistinct speech that parents and friends have learned to interpret after a fashion, but of which other people understand only a fraction. These are the speakers who must repeat and repeat before we can understand them.

Others lack good models. Their parents may be indistinct speakers. Their neighborhood may abound with speakers of other languages who have not mastered English phonemic patterns. Their neighbors may speak a type of English that contrasts unfavorably with the type spoken by those who carry more prestige in the community. Or the models may be satisfactory but the child hampered by poor hearing or poor muscular control.

The result is that many adult speakers speak indistinctly, or otherwise ineffectively. The exercises in this book are designed to heighten the contrasts between phonemes, and to develop acceptable and easily intelligible speech. But exercises alone will not do everything. There must be attention to models of good speech, and those models should be the people in the community, in the speaker's own world, whose status seems assured. The student should not assume that teachers and professors necessarily constitute the best models. Teachers and professors range from the indistinct to the pedantically exaggerated, but some of them qualify. Sometimes another student may serve as a model. Certainly there will be several people in your own personal world with whose speech you can compare your own. You should not, of course, copy slavishly, but you can and should make intelligent use of whatever models are available.

For the foreigner who has learned another language before English, all that has been said thus far, and more, is true. The foreigner has adapted his hearing and his vocal habits to the phonemic pattern of his native language. He listens to differences which are significant in that language, and does not listen to those that don't matter. In English he must learn that different things matter and don't matter. If he is Italian he must start listening for the difference between *seat* and *sit,* a difference that he can ignore in Italian. If he is Japanese he must listen for the differences between *heel, feel,* and *wheel,* differences that he can ignore in Japanese. If he is Spanish he must learn the difference between *gate* and *get,* a difference which he can ignore in Spanish.

The foreigner often has difficult in securing native models, since he often lacks native contacts. In our large universities there is an understandable tendency for Latin Americans to congregate with other Latin Americans and to speak Spanish most of the time, for Filipinos to congregate with those Filipinos who speak their own language. On the other hand, the lone Finn or Icelander is likely to make greater progress with English because he has fewer people who speak his own language to rely on. If the Latin American can develop more English-speaking contacts, as the Icelander is usually forced to do, his progress in English will probably be accelerated.

In using the exercises which constitute the bulk of this book, always begin by contrasting the sound you are trying to perfect with other sounds. You will find many exercises in which the words are arranged in contrasting pairs. Practice them first in pairs, in order to heighten the contrast. Later you may practice them in columns, in order to work for uniformity. The other exercises, those not arranged in pairs, are also designed for practice toward uniformity, since each sound is presented in a variety of phonemic contexts. Listen carefully at all times. Rote repetition will do you no good. You must actively criticize your pronunciation as you go along.

Part II

CONSONANTS

Lip Consonants

Three consonants, [p], [b], and [m], require closed lips. [p] and [b] are stop consonants; both lips and soft-palate valve must be momentarily closed. [m] is a nasal continuant, with closed lips, but with the soft-palate valve open. See Fig. 1 and Fig. 2 below.

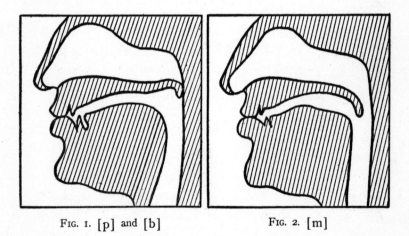

FIG. 1. [p] and [b]   FIG. 2. [m]

The vocal bands vibrate for [b] and [m], but not for [p]. English [p], at the beginning of stressed syllables, as in *play* and *appeal,* requires more breath pressure than [b], or than [p] in other positions, as in *spade, apple,* and *cup.* Lip pressure must be increased to offset the stronger breath pressure. In Exercise

15

1, make [p] voiceless and vigorous; make [b] voiced and only moderately vigorous.

1: Initial [p] and [b]

[p]	[b]	[p]	[b]
peach	beach	pit	bit
pace	base	pest	best
patch	batch	park	bark
pall	ball	puff	buff
poor	boor	perch	birch
pie	buy	pound	bound

2: Initial [pl] and [bl]; [pr] and [br]

[p]	[b]	[p]	[b]
plead	bleed	preach	breech
plays	blaze	prim	brim
plank	blank	pressed	breast
plot	blot	prude	brewed
plush	blush	pride	bride
plight	blight	prow	brow

3: Medial and final [p] and [b]

[p]	[b]	[p]	[b]
rip	rib	tap	tab
mop	mob	rope	robe
cup	cub	tripe	tribe
staple	stable	crumple	crumble
ample	amble	maple	Mabel
rapid	rabid	calipre	calibre

4: Initial [p]

peach, pill, paste, pet, pat, pass, palm, park, pot, pour, pose, punch, push, pool, perch, pine, poise, pound.

5: Initial [pl]

plead, please, plink, play, pled, plan, plank, plot, plod, plum, plush, plunder, plug, plume, ply, plight, plow.

6: Initial [sp]

speed, speak, spin, space, spell, spent, span, spark, spot, sport, spoke, spun, spoon, spur, spy, spoil, spout.

7: Initial [spl]

spleen, split, splint, splinter, splay, splendid, splash, splatter, splotch, splutter, splice.

8: Initial [pr]

preach, prim, prick, prig, pray, praise, press, prayer, prank, prop, prawn, probe, proof, prude, pride, price, proud.

9: Initial [spr]

spree, sprint, spring, spray, sprain, spread, sprang, sprocket, sprawl, sprung, spruce, spry, sprite, sprout.

10: Final [p]

sweep, trip, grape, step, snap, drop, warp, slope, cup, droop, chirp, ripe, help, scalp, lisp, grasp, imp, camp, bump.

11: Medial [p]

people, dipper, maple, reptile, apple, sharpen, copper, corporal, couple, coupon, ripen, captain, optimist, crumple.

12: [p] sentences

He put a piece of pie at each place.
The Presbyterian preacher approved the plan.
The captain captured a porcupine near the pond.
The piano player plodded across the plowed field.
The upper part of the plum tree was full of plums.

13: Initial [b]

bean, busy, bake, bear, best, bank, bark, borrow, ball, bone, buff, book, boom, burst, bind, bite, bound, boy, boil.

14: Initial [bl]

bleed, bliss, blame, bled, blare, black, blot, blow, blown, blush, bluff, blood, bloom, blurt, blight, blouse.

15: Initial [br]

brief, brick, brain, break, bread, brand, broad, broke, brush, brook, broom, bruise, bright, brown, broil.

16: Final [b]

rib, glib, babe, web, slab, grab, squab, sob, robe, rub, scrub, tube, cube, curb, disturb, tribe, imbibe, bulb, absorb.

17: Medial [b]

cabin, rabbit, barber, turbine, cabbage, cubic, object, obsolete, absorb, absurd, lobster, hubcap, lumber, asbestos, elbow, timber, able, umbrella, combine, sunburn, textbook.

18: [b] sentences

The big basket was full of tulip bulbs.
They built a cabin behind the brown barn.
The boy was born in Brooklyn in February.
He borrowed a bucket to bail out the boat.
Lobsters and crabs can be found in the bay.

In contrasting [b] and [m] make sure that the breath is completely stopped for [b], and that it comes easily through your nose for [m].

19: Initial [b] and [m]

[b]	[m]	[b]	[m]
bean	mean	bait	mate
bill	mill	bend	mend
bat	mat	bark	mark
boss	moss	bone	moan
boor	moor	bound	mound
birth	mirth	bind	mind

20: Medial [b] and [m]

[b]	[m]	[b]	[m]
ribs	rims	slabs	slams
cubs	comes	robes	roams
ribbed	rimmed	robed	roamed
carbon	Carmen	clabber	clamor
decibel	decimal	bobbing	bombing
jabbing	jamming	cubbing	coming
shabby	chamois	chubby	chummy

21: Final [b] and [m]

[b]	[m]	[b]	[m]
rib	rim	drab	dram
slab	slam	jab	jam
crab	cram	grab	gram
bob	bomb	lobe	loam
robe	roam	rub	rum
cub	come	hub	hum

22: Initial [m]

meet, mean, mist, mint, make, met, melt, match, mask, march, mark, mob, mock, moss, most, mode, much, month, move, mood, mew, mule, mirth, murky, might, mile, mouth, mouse.

23: Initial [sm]

smear, smith, smell, smash, smack, smart, smock, small, smote, smoke, smudge, smug, smooth, smirch, smirk, smile.

24: Final [m]

team, stream, limb, swim, blame, game, them, stem, lamb, slam, farm, charm, bomb, calm, form, storm, foam, dome, comb, plum, thumb, crumb, broom, tomb, firm, term, worm, time, climb.

25: Final [mp]

imp, limp, shrimp, hemp, tramp, damp, lamp, pomp, romp, swamp, pump, plump, thump, lump, clump, hump, jump, stump.

26: Final [mz]

dreams, trims, blames, stems, lambs, farms, bombs, forms, homes, thumbs, drums, booms, terms, germs, dimes, climbs.

27: Final [md]

schemed, skimmed, framed, condemned, jammed, farmed, calmed, warmed, combed, hummed, doomed, termed, rhymed, climbed.

28: Miscellaneous final [m]

film, elm, overwhelm, prism, spasm, chasm, bosom, autumn, album, bottom, column, forum, wisdom, pilgrim, welcome, custom.

29: Medial [m]

remit, cement, simmer, employ, aimless, empty, amber, ample, sample, ominous, combination, armor, omen, umbrella, rumpled, German, torment, ambush, amplitude, armadillo, whimper, animal.

30: [m] sentences

Moss grows among the cement columns.
The German emperor wore cumbersome armor.
Drums and trumpets accompanied the marchers.
The mice moved in from the fields in November.
The fisherman managed to land the enormous salmon.
The major took command of the camel corps at Khartoum.

Lip-Teeth Consonants

The two English lip-teeth consonants, [f] and [v], are made by pressing the lower lip against the upper teeth and forcing breath between the narrow spaces between the teeth. [f] is voiceless, with strong breath pressure. [v] is voiced, with moderate breath pressure. For both sounds the soft-palate valve must remain closed.

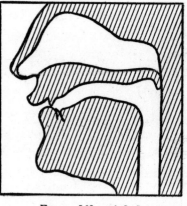

Fig. 3. [f] and [v]

The contrast between stop and explosion for [p] and [b], and continuous emission of the breath for [f] and [v], marks the essential difference between these two groups of sounds. Aim for a light touch of the teeth on the lips. The breath stream should be allowed to come out easily for [f] and [v], without exaggerated facial movements.

31: Initial [p] and [f]

[p]	[f]	[p]	[f]
peel	feel	pin	fin
paid	fade	pair	fair
peasant	pheasant	passion	fashion
pond	fond	Paul	fall
purr	fur	pool	fool
pile	file	position	physician

32: [pr] and [fr], [pl] and [fl]

[p]	[f]	[p]	[f]
pray	fray	plea	flee
prate	freight	play	flay
pressure	fresher	pledge	fledge
prank	frank	plush	flush
pride	fried	plume	flume
prior	fryer	plier	flier

33: Final [p] and [f]

[p]	[f]	[p]	[f]
leap	leaf	cheap	chief
snip	sniff	whip	whiff
lap	laugh	cap	calf
cup	cuff	hoop	hoof
wipe	wife	stripe	strife

34: Medial [p] and [f]

[p]	[f]	[p]	[f]
camper	camphor	puppy	puffy
supper	suffer	captain	caftan
proper	proffer	copper	coffer
wept	weft	apt	aft
dipper	differ	wrapped	raft

35: Initial [f]

feet, feast, fierce, film, fist, faith, phase, fed, felt, fat, fan, far, farm, fond, fog, form, four, foam, fold, foot, full, food, fool, few, fumes, fur, firm, five, foil, found.

36: Initial [fr]

freeze, fringe, frame, phrase, friend, fresh, frank, frock, frog, froth, fraud, froze, fruit, fry, fright, frown, frowzy.

37: Initial [fl]

fleet, fling, flame, flesh, flat, flag, flock, flog, flaw, floor, float, flood, flew, flute, flirt, flight, flout, flounce.

38: Final [f]

beef, thief, stiff, cliff, safe, chafe, deaf, chef, laugh, half, off, cough, loaf, puff, tough, hoof, proof, surf, strife, sylph, elf, shelf, golf, gulf, wolf, Ralph, Randolph, triumph.

39: Final [ft] and [fs]

briefed, drift, chafed, theft, draft, soft, loafed, puffed, roofed, knifed, reefs, cliffs, safes, chefs, laughs, coughs, loafs, bluffs, roofs, proofs, turfs, fifes, wife's, coifs.

40: Medial [f]

sphere, sphinx, spherical, puffy, wafer, suffer, profit, camphor, coffin, differ, defend, shuffle, surface, confection, sniffle, infest, raffle, refuse, reference, rifle, trifle.

41: [f] sentences

Rudolph set his feet firmly on the flat shelf.

The strange fowl was covered with tough feathers.

A heavy fog came into the forest from the gulf.

The fighting men defended the fort with their rifles.

The freezing weather froze the fruit trees on the bluff.

[v] is the voiced counterpart of [f]. Like [f], it is formed with the lower lip resting lightly against the upper teeth, in contrast to [b] in which upper and lower lips are pressed firmly together.

42: Initial [b] and [v]

[b]	[v]	[b]	[v]
beer	veer	berry	very
bail	veil	banish	vanish
best	vest	bolt	volt
boat	vote	bile	vile
burst	versed	bicker	vicar
bigger	vigor	bough	vow

43: Final and medial [b] and [v]

[b]	[v]	[b]	[v]
grebe	grieve	robe	rove
dub	dove	verb	verve
Serb	serve	curb	curve
marble	marvel	ribbon	riven
cupboard	covered	rabble	ravel
sybil	civil	harbored	Harvard

44: Initial [f] and [v]

[f]	[v]	[f]	[v]
feel	veal –	fan	van
fat	vat –	folly	volley –
fail	veil	fine	vine
fault	vault	first	versed
file	vile	foil	voile
fowl	vowel	foist	voiced

45: Final [f] and [v]

[f]	[v]	[f]	[v]
leaf	leave	grief	grieve
calf	calve	half	halve
knife	knive	life	live
shelf	shelve	waif	wave
surf	serve	plaintiff	plaintive

46: Medial [f] and [v]

[f]	[v]	[f]	[v]
wafer	waiver	shuffle	shovel
surface	service	define	divine
sniffle	snivel	infest	invest
raffle	ravel	refuse	reviews
reference	reverence	rifle	rival

47: Initial [v]

veal, veer, vivid, victim, veil, vase, vague, vest, vent, veteran, vat, van, vacuum, vast, varnish, vaunt, vault, vote, vogue, vermin, virtue, verse, verge, vice, vine, vow, vowel.

48: Final [v]

leave, weave, give, live, brave, save, shave, have, starve, carve, drove, stove, above, glove, move, prove, nerve, serve, curve, five, dive, drive, twelve, valve, involve, revolve.

49: Final [vz]

eaves, gives, caves, starves, carves, droves, stoves, loves, gloves, moves, grooves, nerves, curves, dives, drives, knives.

50: Final [vd]

grieved, lived, raved, slaved, carved, starved, roved, shoved, moved, proved, served, curved, thrived, solved, revolved.

51: Medial [v]

even, evil, given, gravy, haven, heaven, Denver, cavern, tavern, scavenge, gavel, anvil, marvel, carving, cover, hover, civil, lover, Harvard, heavy, culvert, converse, divide, evade.

52: [v] sentences

The veteran lived on Seventh Avenue.
Mr. Vernon taught Slavic languages at Harvard.
He wiped the gravy from his vest with his sleeve.
The visitors marveled at the view from Denver.
The thieves drove behind the tavern and vanished.
Evan gave the visitors a choice of veal or venison.

Lip-Back Consonants

Two consonants are formed with the lips closely rounded and the back of the tongue raised. These are the glides [w] and [ʍ], which are not static, but which take off from the diagrammed position and move toward the position of the following vowel.

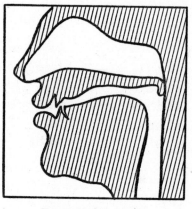

FIG. 4. [w] and [ʍ]

[w] is voiced; [ʍ] is voiceless, a development from the combination [hw], with which it freely alternates. Not all English speakers maintain the distinction between [ʍ] and [w]; many use only [w]. Some speakers maintain the distinction only at the beginning of stressed syllables, but use only [w] when the syllable is unstressed. Note that both [w] and [ʍ] require close rounding of the lips. The teeth should not touch the lips as they do for [f] and [v]. For distinctness the speaker should pronounce [w] and [ʍ] quickly and vigorously, making a rapid transition to the following vowel.

53: [v] and [w]

[v]	[w]	[v]	[w]
veal	weal	veil	wail
vicar	wicker	vary	wary
vain	wane	vent	went
vend	wend	verse	worse
vest	west	vine	wine
viper	wiper	visor	wiser

54: [f] and [ʍ]

[f]	[ʍ]	[f]	[ʍ]
feel	wheel	fizz	whizz
fees	wheeze	fare	where
fail	whale	fen	when
feather	whether	fact	whacked
fine	whine	file	while
furl	whirl	fight	white

55: [w] and [ʍ]

[w]	[ʍ]	[w]	[ʍ]
wear	where	witch	which
wet	whet	wither	whither
weather	whether	wail	whale
watt	what	wax	whacks
wine	whine	wile	while
were	whir	world	whirled
wen	when	wish	whish
weal	wheel	wight	white
way	whey	wary	wherry

56: [b], [v], and [w]

[b]	[v]	[w]
bail	veil	wail
beer	veer	weir
bent	vent	went
burst	versed	worst
bile	vile	wile
bind	vined	wined

57: [w], [ʍ], [f], and [v]

[w]	[ʍ]	[f]	[v]
weal	wheel	feel	veal
wail	whale	fail	veil
wary	wherry	ferry	very
wile	while	file	vile
wine	whine	fine	vine

58: Initial [w]

weed, wield, witch, wish, wave, wait, web, wedge, wax, wag, wasp, watch, warm, warn, wove, woke, one, once, wonder, wolf, wool, were, worm, worth, wipe, wide, wire, wound.

59: [tw], [dw], and [kw]

tweed, tweezers, twitch, twin, twain, twelve, twirl, twine, dwindle, dwelling, dwarf, queen, queer, quick, quaint, quake, quest, quell, quack, qualms, quart, quote, quite, quiet, choir.

60: [sw] and [skw]

sweep, swim, sway, swept, swell, swam, swamp, swan, swore, swollen, swoop, swerve, swirl, swine, squeeze, squint, squid, square, squab, squash, squaw, squall, squirt, squirrel, squire.

61: Medial [w]

unwieldy, herewith, eastward, await, unwind, therewith, awoke, westward, reward, firewood, unworthy, northward, tapeworm, earthworm, northwest, equipment, aquatic, Norwood, halfway.

62: Initial and medial [ʍ]

wheel, wheat, wheeze, whip, whim, whiff, whinny, whisk, which, whisper, whey, whale, whet, when, whelk, whack, what, wharf, whir, whirl, white, whine, while, pinwheel, buckwheat, bullwhip, somewhat, anywhere, somewhere, elsewhere, nowhere.

63: [w] and [ʍ] sentences

The exhausted whale went aground near the wharf.

The horse whinnied when the boys whispered his name.

Mr. Wentworth couldn't find the wheelbarrow anywhere.

The squall drove the white boats against the wooden dock.

The water spaniel chased the squirrel into the wheat field.

Tongue-Teeth Consonants

For [θ] and [ð] the tip of the tongue must touch the front teeth. It may protrude slightly between them, or lightly touch the back of the upper teeth. Both sounds are frictional: [θ] voiceless, with strong breath pressure; [ð] voiced, with moderate pressure. [θ] is often confused with [t], [f], or [s]; [ð], with [d], [v], or [z].

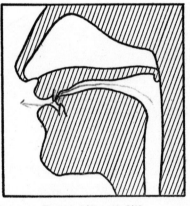

FIG. 5. [θ] and [ð]

For [t] and [d] the tongue must firmly touch the upper gum ridge, not the teeth. For [s] and [z] the tongue tip must be pulled back from the upper teeth, or anchored on the lower gums below the lower teeth. For [f] and [v] the tongue must keep back out of the way, allowing the lower lip to touch the upper teeth. In the following exercises concentrate your attention on touching the tip of the tongue lightly against the teeth for [θ] and [ð].

64: Initial [t] and [θ]

[t]	[θ]	[t]	[θ]
team	theme	tin	thin
tick	thick	tank	thank
taught	thought	torn	thorn
tie	thigh	tree	three
trill	thrill	tread	thread
true	through	trice	thrice

65: Final [t] and [θ]

[t]	[θ]	[t]	[θ]
sheet	sheath	pit	pith
pat	path	rat	wrath
fort	forth	brought	broth
boat	both	boot	booth
toot	tooth	dirt	dearth
tilt	tilth	welt	wealth

66: Medial [t] and [θ]

[t]	[θ]	[t]	[θ]
eater	ether	pity	pithy
metal	methyl	nutting	nothing
heats	heaths	fates	faiths
debts	deaths	tents	tenths
hearts	hearths	droughts	drouths

67: Initial [d] and [ð]

[d]	[ð]	[d]	[ð]
day	they	den	then
dense	thence	dare	there
Dan	than	dough	though
doze	those	die	thy
dine	thine	dither	thither

68: Final [d] and [ð]

[d]	[ð]	[d]	[ð]
breed	breathe	reed	wreathe
seed	seethe	she'd	sheathe
laid.	lathe	bayed	bathe
tide	tithe	lied	lithe
ride	writhe	side	scythe

69: Medial [d] and [ð]

[d]	[ð]	[d]	[ð]
breeder	breather	breeding	breathing
rider	writher	riding	writhing
header	heather	wordy	worthy
fodder	father	ladder	lather
seeds	seethes	tides	tithes
'rides	writhes	sides	scythes

70: [θ] and [ð] sentences

Ruth and Edith have tickets to the theatre.

The rabbit lived in a thicket of thorn bushes.

They went bathing on the thirtieth of August.

Think the thought through till you find the truth.

Neither his mother nor his brother could breathe with comfort.

The author lived at the corner of Fifth Avenue and Sixth Street.

The snakes slithered hither and thither in the green heather.

For [f] touch the teeth with your lower lip; for [θ] touch the teeth with the tip of your tongue.

71: Initial [f] and [θ]

[f]	[θ]	[f]	[θ]
free	three	freeze	threes
fin	thin	fret	threat
frill	thrill	fresh	thresh
Fred	thread	fought	thought
first	thirst	froze	throes
furred	third	furrow	thorough

72: Final [f] and [θ]

[f]	[θ]	[f]	[θ]
reef	wreath	sheaf	sheath
deaf	death	laugh	lath
half	hath	oaf	oath
loaf	loath	roof	Ruth

73: Medial [f] and [θ]

[f]	[θ]	[f]	[θ]
offer	author	leafy	Lethe
deafly	deathly	roofless	ruthless
miffs	myths	laughs	laths
oafs	oaths	roofs	Ruth's

74: [v] and [ð]

[v]	[ð]	[v]	[ð]
vat	that	van	than
vine	thine	vow	thou
lave	lathe	clove	clothe
rive	writhe	live	lithe
lever	leather	fervor	further
laves	lathes	rives	writhes
loaves	loathes	sheaves	sheathes

75: [f], [v], [θ], and [ð] sentences

They caught a thin fish with three fins.

His religious fervor would carry him no further.

The northern weather was rather severe for Mother.

Every good housewife loathes stale loaves of bread.

They would rather swim in the river than in the lake.

On the fourth Thursday she cleaned the house thoroughly.

For [s] and [z] keep the tongue tip away from the teeth.

76: Initial [s] and [θ]

[s]	[θ]	[s]	[θ]
seem	theme	sin	thin
sick	thick	sing	thing
sought	thought	sank	thank
surd	third	some	thumb
sigh	thigh	size	thighs

77: Final and medial [s] and [θ]

[s]	[θ]	[s]	[θ]
miss	myth	race	wraith
face	faith	lass	lath
pass	path	Norse	north
force	fourth	truce	truth
mouse	mouth	worse	worth
useful	youthful	answers	anthers

78: Final [z] and [ð]

[z]	[ð]	[z]	[ð]
breeze	breathe	tease	teethe
sees	seethe	lays	lathe
baize	bathe	ties	tithe
lies	lithe	rise	writhe
sighs	scythe	close	clothe

79: Medial [z] and [ð]

[z]	[ð]	[z]	[ð]
wizard	withered	breezing	breathing
teasing	teething	seizing	seething
rising	writhing	closing	clothing
breezed	breathed	teased	teethed
seized	seethed	closed	clothed

80: [θ] and [ð]

[θ]	[ð]	[θ]	[ð]
teeth	teethe	sheath	sheathe
wreath	wreathe	sooth	soothe
loath	loathe	ether	either

81: [s], [z], [θ], and [ð] sentences

The youthful athletes dashed across the path.

The rusty old lathe was worse than worthless.

The lizard slithered along the southeast wall.

The withered old wizard lived in a filthy cave.

The writhing snake had a small mouse in its mouth.

The clothing store on Seventh Street held a closing-out sale.

82: Initial [θ]

thief, theme, theory, thick, thing, thimble, theft, thank, thought, thorn, thumb, thunder, third, Thursday, thyroid, thousand, thwart, three, thrill, thread, thrash, throb, throng, throat.

83: Medial and final [θ]

ether, author, method, healthy, panther, synthetic, hawthorn, truthful, lengthen, myths, births, deaths, beneath, faith, path, moth, both, tooth, earth, mouth, width, eighth, twelfth, warmth.

84: [θ] sentences

The thief stole a thousand dollars in Southampton.

The thunderstorm damaged the hawthorn trees in the south.

The author took an Indian myth for the theme of his story.

The stealthy panther threatened the safety of the settlement.

Theodore and Ethel have just had their eighteenth birthdays.

The length of the bathroom was thirteen feet and three inches.

85: [ð]

these, this, then, there, they, that, though, breathe, bathe, clothe, smooth, scythe, father, mother, bother, gather, wither, weather, either, northern, southern, breathed, clothed, smoothed, breathes, seethes, bathes, loathes, smooths, mouths.

86: [ð] sentences

Mother tried to soothe the teething baby.

They gathered the feathers rather quickly.

My father bequeathed his leather business to me.

Breathing was difficult and we almost smothered.

Southern weather is therefore pleasanter than northern.

The brothers left their clothing on shore and went bathing.

Gum-Ridge Consonants

For English [t], [d], and [n] the tip of the tongue must touch the upper gums. [t] is voiceless; [d] and [n] are voiced. For [n] the soft-palate valve must be open; for [t] and [d] it must be shut. Don't allow the tongue tip to touch the upper front teeth except immediately before or after [θ] or [ð], as in *eighth, tenth, width, Southdown,* and *withdraw.*

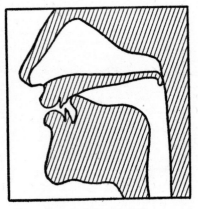

Fig. 6. [t] and [d]

To avoid a foreign-sounding dental articulation of [t] and [d], practice Exercises 64 to 69 in reverse order. Pull the tongue back slightly as you change from a [θ]-word to a [t]-word, and from a [ð]-word to a [d]-word. Then practice Exercise 87 rapidly. Keep pulling the tongue back, but without curling up the tip. Keep working at the new placement of the tongue tip at regular practice sessions till the new habit becomes established.

87: Gum-ridge articulation

too	too	too	too	too	doo	doo	doo	doo	doo
toe	toe	toe	toe	toe	doe	doe	doe	doe	doe
taw	taw	taw	taw	taw	daw	daw	daw	daw	daw
tah	tah	tah	tah	tah	dah	dah	dah	dah	dah
noo	noo	noo	noo	noo	loo	loo	loo	loo	loo
noe	noe	noe	noe	noe	loe	loe	loe	loe	loe
naw	naw	naw	naw	naw	law	law	law	law	law
nah	nah	nah	nah	nah	lah	lah	lah	lah	lah

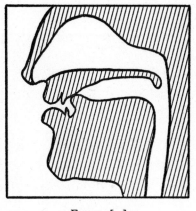

FIG. 7 [n]

Keep the tongue tip away from the teeth. Keep [t] voiceless and [d] voiced.

88: Initial [t] and [d]

[t]	[d]	[t]	[d]
team	deem	tin	din
tame	dame	ten	den
tell	dell	tank	dank
tore	door	toes	doze
tusk	dusk	time	dime
tomb	doom	town	down

89: Final [t] and [d]

[t]	[d]	[t]	[d]
feet	feed	hit	hid
fate	fade	debt	dead
sat	sad	heart	hard
knot	nod	brought	broad
but	bud	coat	code
curt	curd	clout	cloud

90: Medial [t] and [d]

[t]	[d]	[t]	[d]
bitter	bidder	waiter	wader
writer	rider	pouter	powder
traitor	trader	betting	bedding
shutter	shudder	contemn	condemn

91: Initial [t]

team, teach, tip, tinge, tape, take, ten, Texas, tap, tag, tar, tarnish, top, toxic, toss, torch, toad, tone, tub, tough, took, tour, tomb, term, turf, type, time, toy, toil, tower.

92: Initial [tr] and [tw]

tree, trim, trade, trench, tramp, trod, trawl, troll, trump, troop, try, Troy, trounce, trowel, tweed, tweezers, twitch, twin, twist, twig, twinkle, twain, twelve, twirl, twine, twice.

93: Initial [st] and [str]

steep, stiff, stale, step, staff, stark, stop, stalk, stone, stump, stood, stoop, stern, sturdy, style, stream, strip, stray, stretch, strap, straw, stroll, strung, strife, stride.

94: Final [t]

sweet, grit, freight, threat, flat, part, shot, caught, vote, shut, foot, fruit, hurt, white, quoit, doubt, feast, mist, haste, nest, last, lost, ghost, dust, boost, hoist, mint, paint, went, plant, felt, fault, cult, crypt, slept, act, ached.

95: Medial [t]

meter, pity, litter, waiter, native, metal, debtor, batter, motto, haughty, motive, butter, booty, mighty, loiter, outing, winter, painted, enter, pantry, haunted, hunter, melted, altar, bolted, cultivate, blister, cluster, boosted, oyster, aptitude.

96: [t] sentences

The stream ran between steep stone walls.

The twins played with twelve twisted twigs.

The team made two touchdowns in the first quarter.

The trespasser was trapped in a trench near the turret.

The painting depicted a freight train caught in a snowdrift.

In winter they hunted, but in summer they cultivated potatoes.

Keep your tongue pulled back from your teeth for [d].

97: Initial [d]

deep, deal, dim, ditch, day, date, depth, deaf, dash, dance, dart, dark, dot, dodge, dog, daunt, door, dome, doze, dumb, dust, do, doom, dirt, dirge, dime, dine, doily, doubt.

98: [dr] and [dw]

dream, drift, drill, drape, drain, dredge, dress, drank, draft, drama, drop, drawl, drove, drone, drum, drug, droop, dry, drive, drouth, drown, dwindle, dwell, dwarf, Duane, Dwight.

99: Final [d]

bleed, slid, shade, said, glad, yard, squad, broad, load, mud, should, food, word, pride, void, cloud, cleaned, rained, end, fond, fund, find, found, field, filled, nailed, gnarled, bald, bold, culled, pulled, fooled, curled, mild, oiled, howled.

100: Medial [d]

needle, middle, ladle, medal, paddle, hardly, muddle, idle, curdle, didn't, redden, sadden, garden, sudden, burden, elder, scalding, boulder, order, admiral, indigo, odor, medium, caddy, moderate, under, bidder, trader, shudder, London, candle, bundle.

101: [d] sentences

The admiral tuned in the London radio.
The desk was covered with dust and dirt.
He doubled his wife's bid of six diamonds.
He dreamed he was drifting around in mid air.
Dwight and Hilda cleared the dining room table of dishes.
The trader's address was a small building behind the dock.

For [m] and [n] keep the sound coming freely through your nose. For [n] the tongue tip should touch the upper gums, not the teeth.

102: Initial [m] and [n]

[m]	[n]	[m]	[n]
meal	kneel	mob	knob
mitt	knit	melt	knelt
mail	nail	mote	note
mash	gnash	muzzle	nuzzle
might	night	moose	noose

103: Final [m] and [n]

[m]	[n]	[m]	[n]
beam	bean	grim	grin
lame	lane	hem	hen
ram	ran	foam	phone
dumb	done	loom	loon
firm	fern	lime	line

104: Medial [m] and [n]

[m]	[n]	[m]	[n]
coming	cunning	simmer	sinner
acme	acne	comic	conic
screaming	screening	warming	warning
seems	scenes	gums	guns
termed	turned	warmed	warned

Explode the [d] with moderate vigor; let the [n] come easily through the nose. Make the tongue contact on the gum ridge.

105: Initial [d] and [n]

[d]	[n]	[d]	[n]
deal	kneel	dame	name
dear	near	dash	gnash
debt	net	dumb	numb
dot	knot	dives	knives
doze	nose	down	noun

106: Final [d] and [n]

[d]	[n]	[d]	[n]
skid	skin	seed	scene
red	wren	trade	train
mode	moan	pad	pan
bud	bun	wad	wan
divide	divine	stirred	stern

107: Medial [d] and [n]

[d]	[n]	[d]	[n]
paddle	panel	curdle	kernel
fuddle	funnel	tidy	tiny
cider	signer	body	bonny
medial	menial	rudder	runner
odor	owner	corridor	coroner

108: Initial [n]

knee, need, near, knit, name, nail, net, nest, neck, nap, gnash, knack, knob, knock, gnaw, north, note, nose, numb, nub, none, nook, noose, nerve, nurse, knife, night, noise, now, noun.

109: Initial [sn]

sneeze, sneer, snip, sniff, snail, snake, snare, snap, snatch, snob, snore, snow, snub, snuff, snooze, snipe, snout.

110: Final [n]

clean, green, thin, chin, chain, gain, then, when, plan, scan, barn, wan, swan, gone, born, throne, stone, fun, done, soon, spoon, turn, learn, pine, sign, coin, loin, brown, down.

111: Final [ns] and [nt]

since, wince, fence, sense, dance, chance, once, ounce, bounce, print, hint, paint, quaint, meant, went, aunt, plant, want, gaunt, won't, blunt, front, burnt, pint, point, count.

112: Final [nz] and [nd]

screens, pins, gains, fans, swans, lawns, moans, buns, moons, turns, fines, joins, towns, cleaned, sinned, rained, spend, band, fond, dawned, moaned, shunned, crooned, sound.

113: Medial [n]

panel, kernel, tiny, bonny, menial, runner, funnel, tenor, cunning, sinner, dinner, colony, connect, acne, conic, coroner, canal, venal, penalty, cannibal, ordinary, flannel, anemone.

114: [n] sentences

Green pines grew on the sunny side of the mountain.

The tiny colony was surrounded by native cannibals.

None of the neighbors knew where the nurse had gone.

The tenor snoozed and snored during the intermission.

His new raincoat covered him from his neck to his knees.

They found the stolen spoons in a tin can behind the barn.

Nobody knew if it was nine o'clock or not.

[1]

English [l] is a single phoneme with a variety of forms, or allophones, determined by the phonetic context. All forms are lateral; breath and voice escape over one or both sides of the tongue. Normally the tip of the tongue comes in contact with the gum ridge. Only in the neighborhood of [θ], as in *health* and *athlete,* does it touch the teeth.

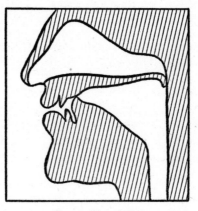

FIG. 8. Clear [l]

Fig. 8 and Fig. 9 illustrate the two main varieties of American English [l]. The clear [l], with the upper surface of the tongue sloping gradually back from the point of contact on the gum ridge, always occurs immediately before a vowel. It may occur at the beginning of a syllable, as in *let, allow,* and *quickly;* or after a consonant, as in *sled, play,* and *acclaim.*

The dark [l], in which the back of the tongue rises slightly toward the soft palate in addition to the contact on the gum ridge, occurs at the ends of words, as in *tell* and *hustle;* and before consonants, as in *told* and *else.* Between vowels, as in *silly* and *hollow,* most Americans use the dark [l], but most Southerners use the clear.

To avoid contact of the tip of the tongue with the teeth, review Exercise 87. In contrasting [l] with [n] in Exercises 115-117, be sure that you lower the soft palate for [n] and keep the sides of the tongue raised. For [l] raise the soft palate but lower the sides of the tongue.

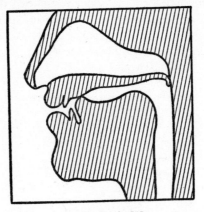

FIG. 9. Dark [l]

115: Initial [n] and [l]

[n]	[l]	[n]	[l]
knit	lit	niece	lease
name	lame	nest	lest
knot	lot	knack	lack
gnaw	law	node	load
null	lull	nook	look
knife	life	noose	loose

116: Final [n] and [l]

[n]	[l]	[n]	[l]
mean	meal	chin	chill
vein	veil	den	dell
fawn	fall	shone	shoal
spoon	spool	fern	furl
churn	churl	coin	coil
pine	pile	whine	while

117: Medial [n] and [l]

[n]	[l]	[n]	[l]
connect	collect	winnow	willow
conic	colic	saunter	psalter
meant	melt	mind	mild
cones	coals	coins	coils
trained	trailed	find	filed

For [d] the sides of the tongue remain up; for [l] they should be lowered to let the breath and the sound out laterally.

118: Initial [d] and [l]

[d]	[l]	[d]	[l]
deep	leap	dim	limb
debt	let	daisy	lazy
dark	lark	dash	lash
dawn	lawn	door	lore
doom	loom	dove	love
dike	like	doubt	lout

119: Final [d] and [l]

[d]	[l]	[d]	[l]
need	kneel	hid	hill
made	mail	shed	shell
node	knoll	food	fool
wood	wool	heard	hurl
proud	prowl	guide	guile
feed	feel	grid	grill
raid	rail	fed	fell
broad	brawl	curd	curl
rude	rule	void	voile
tied	tile	road	roll

120: Medial [d] and [l]

[d]	[l]	[d]	[l]
wooden	woolen	shadow	shallow
incident	insolent	sudden	sullen
modify	mollify	trader	trailer
widow	willow	meadow	mellow
reddish	relish	herds	hurls

121: Initial [l]

leave, least, lisp, link, lame, lake, left, length, lamp, laugh, lark, large, lot, log, loft, lord, loaf, loan, lump, love, look, loom, lose, learn, lurk, life, light, loin, loud.

122: Initial [kl]

clean, cleave, clear, clip, clinch, clay, claim, cleft, cleanse, clap, clash, clot, clock, clog, claw, cloth, close, cloak, clump, clutch, clue, clerk, climb, cloy, cloud, clown.

123: Initial [gl]

glee, gleam, glean, glimpse, glitter, glade, glaze, glen, glare, glad, glass, gloss, glow, globe, gloat, glory, glove, glum, glut, glue, gloomy, glide, glower.

124: Initial [sl]

sleeve, sleep, sleet, sleek, slip, slim, slit, slink, slay, slave, slate, slept, sled, slap, slam, slack, slot, slaughter, slow, slope, slum, slung, sloop, slur, sly, slight, slouch.

For initial [pl], [bl], and [fl], see Exercises 2, 5, 14, 32, and 37.

125: Final [l]

squeal, skill, snail, dwell, shell, shall, snarl, doll, ball, shawl, soul, goal, dull, skull, pull, full, pool, school, mule, pearl, hurl, style, while, broil, spoil, foul, scowl.

126: Final [lt] and [ld]

built, quilt, melt, dealt, fault, vault, bolt, volt, cult, spoilt, shield, spilled, failed, held, snarled, bald, told, gold, dulled, pulled, fooled, world, child, foiled, scowled.

127: Final [ls], [lts], [sl], and [stəl]

else, false, pulse, wilts, melts, waltz, bolts, cults, whistle, wrestle, vessel, castle, parcel, morsel, jostle, muscle, hustle, rehearsal, pencil, cancel, tonsil, pistol, hostile.

128: Final [lz], [ldz], [zl], and [zlz]

feels, skills, gales, shells, snarls, dolls, shawls, shoals, skulls, pulls, schools, mules, pearls, styles, boils, fowls, wields, guilds, welds, scalds, holds, wilds, weasel, drizzle, hazel, dazzle, muzzle, weasels, drizzles, muzzles, nuzzles.

129: [l] plus miscellaneous final consonants

filth, tilth, health, stealth, wealth, silk, milk, bilk, elk, whelk, bulk, sulk, hulk, filch, belch, gulch, sylph, elf, self, shelf, golf, wolf, film, elm, overwhelm.

130: Medial [l]

collect, willow, colic, shallow, wooly, insolent, mellow, sullen, silly, hollow, bellow, alum, color, collar, follow, folly, gallon, pillow, wallet, wallow, salad, solid, palate, swallow, dollar, felon, talent, relay, quality, cylinder.

131: [l] sentences

The swallows collected near the willow tree.

The little lad learned his lessons by lamplight.

They drove their automobile from California to Florida.

They pulled eels and turtles from the pool on the island.

The children squealed and yelled when they heard the bells.

The train whistled for the railroad crossing in the valley.

The Consonant [r]

American English [r] has two main varieties; see the diagrams. Both are glides; the tongue moves quickly from the position to a vowel, or to the position from a preceding vowel.

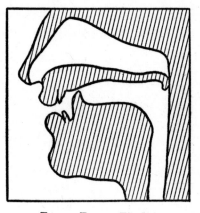

Fig. 10. Tongue-Tip [r]

Some speakers in Eastern New England, the New York City area, and the Coastal South pronounce [r] only when it precedes a vowel, as in *red, three,* and *very* but omit [r] in other positions, as in *far* and *farm.* Consider the preference of your own region of the country.

Those who confuse [w] with [r] will usually get better results by aiming for the tongue-tip [r]; those who confuse [l] with [r], by aiming at the central-tongue [r]. In either position, aim for light but rigorous action of the speech mechanism. Don't prolong [r] to the point at which it begins to sound like a vowel.

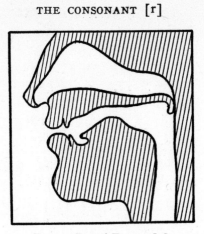

Fig. 11. Central-Tongue [r]

132: Initial [w] and [r]

[w]	[r]	[w]	[r]
weep	reap	wield	reeled
west	rest	witch	rich
wax	racks	wave	rave
wad	rod	wangle	wrangle
one	run	wove	rove
wipe	ripe	wound	round

133: Medial [w] and [r]

[w]	[r]	[w]	[r]
quick	crick	quest	crest
quake	crake	quack	crack
quire	crier	twain	train
tweed	treed	twice	trice
squeak	screak	twill	trill
twist	tryst	away	array

134: Initial [l] and [r]

[l]	[r]	[l]	[r]
leap	reap	leak	reek
lift	rift	lake	rake
late	rate	lavish	ravish
lest	rest	lock	rock
load	road	long	wrong
lime	rhyme	loyal	royal

135: Medial and final [l] and [r]

[l]	[r]	[l]	[r]
play	pray	plod	prod
splint	sprint	blade	brayed
bleed	breed	clash	crash
flute	fruit	cloud	crowd
glazier	grazier	mallow	marrow
palate	parrot	collect	correct

136: [w], [l], and [r]

[w]	[l]	[r]
weep	leap	reap
wink	link	rink
wake	lake	rake
west	lest	rest
wag	lag	rag
watt	lot	rot
wide	lied	ride
quipped	clipped	crypt

137: Initial [r]

reed, reef, reason, rim, rich, ridge, ray, rate, rage, red, rent, wretched, rat, raft, rag, rot, rock, romp, raw, wrong, road, roll, roast, rub, rough, rug, rook, room, ruin, ruse, ripe, right, ride, royal, Royce, round, rouse, rowdy,

138: [pr] and [spr]

preen, preach, prick, prink, pray, praise, precious, press, prank, prod, prong, probe, prose, prove, prune, pride, price, proud, spree, spring, spray, sprang, sprawl, spruce.

139: [br]

breed, breeze, brim, bring, brain, break, bread, brevity, brash, brag, Bronx, broad, broth, broke, brogue, brook, broom, bruise, brood, brine, bright, bride, broil, brown, browse.

140: [fr] and [θr]

freeze, frigid, frame, fresh, fracture, France, frolic, frog, frost, froze, front, fruit, three, thrift, thread, throb, throng, throw, throne, throat, thrust, thrush, threw, thrice.

141: [tr] and [str]

treat, trip, trade, tread, trash, trot, trawl, troll, trump, truth, try, Troy, trout, stream, strip, strain, stress, strap, straw, strong, strode, stroke, stripe, stride, strife.

142: [dr]

dream, drift, drink, dray, drain, dress, dredge, drab, draft, drank, drama, drop, drawn, drawl, drone, drove, drug, drudge, drew, droop, drool, drive, dry, drought, drown.

143: [ʃr]

shriek, shrift, shrill, shrink, shred, shrapnel,
shrank, shrove, shrub, shrug, shrunk, shrewd,
shrine, shroud.

144: [kr] and [skr]

cream, crib, crave, crept, crash, crop, cross, crawl,
crow, crust, crook, crew, cry, crowd, scream, screech,
script, scrimp, scrap, scratch, scrawl, scrawny,
scroll, screw, scruple.

145: [gr]

grief, greed, grim, grill, grin, gray, grace, grape,
grand, grass, grotto, grove, growth, groan, grub,
gruff, grunt, grew, groom, groove, grime, grind,
groin, ground, grouse.

146: [r] between vowels

hero, zero, weary, dairy, fairy, wary, merry,
berry, very, marry, carrot, narrow, borrow, sorry,
forest, foreign, moral, Laura, warrior, story, glory,
soaring, flooring, courage, turret, boorish, tourist,
fury, purity, fiery, flowery.

147: [r] before consonants

beard, weird, fierce, scarce, cared, spares, heart,
farce, cart, shark, barn, alarm, fork, north, sword,
force, scorn, moored, tours, assured, fires, tired, iron,
hired, scoured.

148: Final [r]

fear, sheer, cheer, spear, fair, chair, care, dare, far, car, star, scar, for, corps, door, four, floor, boor, moor, poor, sure, tour, fire, spire, tire, flower, sour, shower.

149: [r] sentences

The runaway rapidly reached the rugged rocks.

The greedy hog upset the great barrel of grain.

The preacher presented the prize to the sprinter.

The children crawled under the crib and screamed.

He trained the trumpet vine to travel up the trellis.

The tourist traveled to Colorado, Missouri, and Oregon.

The horses ran through the barn door to the garden.

The committee purchased fireworks for the celebration.

Laura and Florence went riding last Saturday afternoon.

Hard-Palate Consonants

[s]

For [s] we must force a narrow stream of breath between the tongue and the upper gum ridge, and then direct this stream against the edges of the teeth. Since individual jaws and teeth are shaped differently, different people must make slight differ-

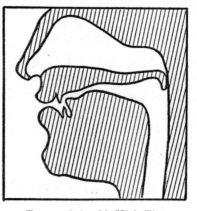

Fig. 12. [s] with High Tip

ences in the adjustment. Fig. 12 and Fig. 13 show the approximate positions which most often produce satisfactory results. In both, we narrow the air passage by placing the tongue close to the upper gum ridge. In both, we pull the tongue far enough away from the upper teeth and the cutting edges of both upper and lower teeth. In both, we pull the sides of the tongue in toward the center, so that the upper surface of the tongue becomes grooved from front to back.

If the tongue tip comes too far forward, and comes too close to the cutting edges of the teeth, [s] is likely to whistle. If the tip actually touches the teeth, [θ] may be heard instead. If we pull the tongue too far back, and lose the center groove, [s] will sound too much like [ʃ]. Those who suffer from high-frequency deafness will also confuse [s] with [f].

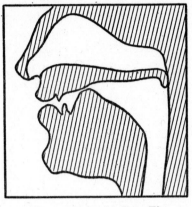

FIG. 13. [s] with Low Tip

In practising, aim for one of the positions diagrammed above; then aim for the other. Then concentrate your practice on the position which produces a more satisfactory sound or more comfort in production. Listen intently for the contrasts featured in the exercises.

150: Initial [θ] and [s]

[θ]	[s]	[θ]	[s]
theme	seem	thin	sin
thick	sick	thing	sing
thank	sank	thought	sought
thole	soul	thumb	some
third	surd	thigh	sigh
thighs	size	thwart	swart
thimble	symbol	thill	sill
think	sink	thicken	sicken
thong	song	thunder	sunder

151: Medial and final [θ] and [s]

[θ]	[s]	[θ]	[s]
myth	miss	wraith	race
faith	face	lath	lass
path	pass	north	Norse
forth	force	truth	truce
growth	gross	worth	worse
mouth	mouse	youthful	useful

In Exercises 152 and 153 concentrate your attention on stretching the tongue lengthwise for [s] and sidewise for [ʃ]. For [s], try to feel the grooving, but avoid letting the tongue tip get too close to the teeth.

152: Initial [ʃ] and [s]

[ʃ]	[s]	[ʃ]	[s]
sheet	seat	shield	sealed
shift	sift	shame	same
shelf	self	shack	sack
shock	sock	shoal	soul
shun	sun	shoot	suit
shine	sign	shower	sour

153: Final and medial [ʃ] and [s]

[ʃ]	[s]	[ʃ]	[s]
leash	lease	swish	Swiss
mesh	mess	clash	class
push	puss	fished	fist
partial	parcel	rushed	rust
erasure	eraser	fashion	fasten
mashes	masses	leashes	leases

154: Initial [f] and [s]

[f]	[s]	[f]	[s]
feet	seat	fit	sit
favor	savor	fed	said
fang	sang	foggy	soggy
ford	sword	fold	sold
fur	sir	fight	sight
foil	soil	found	sound

155: Initial [fl] and [sl]

[fl]	[sl]	[fl]	[sl]
fleet	sleet	flick	slick
fling	sling	fled	sled
flake	slake	flag	slag
flash	slash	flow	slow
flap	slap	flung	slung
fly	sly	flight	slight

156: Final and medial [f] and [s]

[f]	[s]	[f]	[s]
leaf	lease	chafe	chase
turf	terse	buff	bus
elf	else	knife	nice
lift	list	leafed	least
left	lest	laughed	last
coughed	cost	buffed	bust

157: Initial [s]

seem, seed, seek, sift, silt, sink, say, safe, sail, sake, self, sent, sell, sat, sand, sank, solve, sod, sock, soft, sought, song, soap, sold, soak, some, such, sunk, soot, soup, soon, serve, search, surge, sight, sound, sour.

158: Final [s]

fleece, niece, lease, miss, bliss, hiss, ace, place,
brace, bless, dress, yes, pass, brass, glass, farce, moss,
toss, loss, dose, us, fuss, puss, moose, loose, goose,
verse, curse, worse, ice, price, twice, voice, choice,
mouse, house.

159: [s] between vowels

receipt, creases, kisses, hissing, aces, placing,
racer, lacing, classify, pacify, lassitude, possible,
mossy, glossy, bosses, doses, fussing, trousseau,
gruesome, vices, voices.

160: Initial [sp], [spr], [spl], and [sf]

speed, spin, spade, spell, span, spark, spot, sport,
spawn, spoke, sponge, spoon, spurt, spine, spoil,
spout, spree, spring, spray, spread, sprang, sprawl,
sprung, spry, sprout, spleen, split, splendid, splash,
sphere, sphinx, spherical.

161: Final and medial [sp], [ps], and [sps]

crisp, gasp, clasp, wasp, cusp, leaps, grips, tapes,
lapse, carps, tops, warps, ropes, coops, types, wispy,
aspen, waspish, hospital, bicuspid, tipsy, lapses,
topside, lisps, grasps, cusps.

162: [sw]

sweep, Swede, swift, swindle, sway, swain, swept,
swell, swam, swank, swan, swallow, sworn, swarm,
swollen, swum, swoop, swerve, swine.

163: Initial [st] and [str]

steam, sting, stage, step, stack, start, stock, stall,
stone, stuff, stood, stool, stern, style, stout, stream,

string, straight, stretch, strap, strong, stroke, strung, strew, stride.

164: Final [st], [ts], and [sts]

feast, mist, waste, best, past, lost, boast, just, boost, first, iced, moist, oust, beats, wits, gates, lets, gnats, parts, yachts, thoughts, oats, cuts, puts, boots, hurts, nights, quoits, doubts, feasts, lists, pastes, bests, blasts, costs, ghosts, trusts, boosts, bursts, hoists, ousts.

165: Medial [st]

feasting, eastern, blister, listed, tasting, wasted, pester, tested, aster, nasty, roster, costume, frosty, costing, boasted, toaster, muster, boosting, roosted, ousted, hoisted.

166: Initial [sl]

sleep, sleeve, sleet, slim, slid, sling, slave, slate, slept, sled, slam, slash, slot, slosh, slow, slope, slump, sludge, slush, sloop, sluice, slur, slide, slight, slouch.

167: Final and medial [sl] and [ls]

bristle, whistle, basal, vessel, wrestle, tassel, castle, parcel, jostle, morsel, muscle, hustle, else, false, pulse, Elsie, calcium, ulcer, Olson, also, balsam, Nelson, Tulsa.

168: [sm]

smear, smith, smell, smelt, smash, smack, smart, smock, small, smote, smoke, smudge, smug, smooth, smirch, smirk, smite, smile, Christmas, isthmus, basement, iceman, gunsmith.

169: [sn] and [ns]

sneak, snip, snake, snare, snag, snob, snore, snub, snoop, snipe, snout, wince, fence, dance, once, bounce, listen, hasten, lesson, fasten, parson, loosen, person, bison, moisten, winces, fences, answer, mustn't, moistens, bouncing.

170: Initial [sk], [skr], and [skw]

scheme, skip, skate, sketch, scalp, scarf, Scotch, scoff, scald, scope, skull, scoop, skirt, sky, scout, screen, script, scrape, scratch, scrawl, scroll, screw, scribe, squeeze, squid, square, squadron, squall, squirt, squire.

171: Final and medial [sk], [ks], and [sks]

disk, desk, mask, husk, leaks, mix, aches, vex, backs, box, walks, chokes, flux, books, dukes, works, dikes, fixes, accent, boxer, coaxes, Tuxedo, irksome, frisks, desks, masked, tusks.

172: [s] sentences

Several swimmers swam past the ropes.
The spy stole silently away to the south.
Esther wore her new spring suit on Easter.
They stayed at the tennis courts till dusk.
The spherical sculpture fascinated the youngster.
The scientist made a systematic search for the fossil.
The scouts forced their way through mists and swamps.

[z]

[z] is produced with essentially the same choice of tongue positions as [s], but with the tongue muscles slightly relaxed, and

the vocal bands vibrating. Examine Figs. 12 and 13 at the beginning of the [s] section again. If you keep the tongue high and pulled back for [s], you should do likewise for [z]. If you put the tongue tip below the lower teeth for [s], you should do the same for [z].

The contrast between [ð] and [z] is like that between [θ] and [s]; for [θ] and [ð] the tongue tip must touch the teeth; for [s] and [z] it must not. The contrast between [v] and [z] is like that between [f] and [s]; for [f] and [v] the lower lip must touch the upper teeth; for [s] and [z] it must stay down out of the way. The contrast between [ʒ] and [z] is like that between [ʃ] and [s]; for [ʃ] and [ʒ] the tongue must be pulled further back and flattened from side to side; for [s] and [z] it must be grooved down the midline.

173: [ð] and [z]

[ð]	[z]	[ð]	[z]
breathe	breeze	teethe	tease
bathe	bays	lathe	lays
lithe	lies	clothe	close
teethed	teased	breathed	breezed
breathing	breezing	clothed	closed
seething	seizing	writhing	rising
clothing	closing	withered	wizard

174: [v] and [z]

[v]	[z]	[v]	[z]
veal	zeal	vest	zest
eve	ease	brave	braise
rave	raise	slave	slays
gave	gaze	have	has
starve	stars	rove	rose
dove	does	dive	dies
evil	easel	weevil	weasel
haven't	hasn't	divert	dessert

Few minimal contrasts between [ʒ] and [z] occur in English. Most of the pairs in this exercise involve other phonemic contrasts as well as those between [ʒ] and [z].

175: [ʒ] and [z]

[ʒ]	[z]	[ʒ]	[z]
rouge	ruse	seizure	Caesar
composure	composer	glazier	glazer
measure	mezzanine	pleasure	pleasant
inclosure	incloses	usual	usable
vision	visible	division	divisible
revision	revises	elision	Elizabeth

In contrasting [z] with [s] bear in mind that [z] should be voiced, at the end as well as at the beginning of words. Remember, too, that for [z] the muscles should be slightly more relaxed, and the breath pressure slightly less, than for [s].

176: [s] and [z]

[s]	[z]	[s]	[z]
seal	zeal	sip	zip
sink	zinc	sown	zone
niece	knees	hiss	his
pace	pays	sparse	spars
source	sores	dose	doze
fuss	fuzz	deuce	dues
purse	purrs	rice	rise

177: Initial [z]

zeal, zebra, zenith, zero, zinc, zinnia, zipper, zither, zigzag, zany, Zanesville, zealous, zephyr, zest, Zanzibar, zodiac, zoology, zoo, zoom, Zulu, xylophone.

178: Final [z]

breeze, freeze, trees, is, fizz, his, phrase, daze, gaze, fez, says, has, jazz, because, gauze, flaws, stores, those, doze, buzz, fuzz, does, ooze, bruise, whose, spurs, stirs, hers, prize, buys, size, boys, toys, noise, browse, rouse, cows.

179: Final [bz], [mz], and [vz]

ribs, babes, webs, grabs, mobs, absorbs, globes, rubs, tubes, verbs, tribes, seems, limbs, blames, hems, hams, arms, bombs, forms, foams, plums, rooms, germs, times, leaves, gives, saves, valves, carves, droves, loves, grooves, serves, knives.

180: Final [ðz] and [dz]

breathes, wreathes, sheathes, bathes, lathes, baths, loathes, smooths, writhes, mouths, reeds, lids, aids, beds, pads, cards, gods, roads, floods, moods, birds, rides, clouds.

181: Final [nz] and [lz]

cleans, shins, brains, cleanse, fans, barns, lawns, tones, shuns, boons, turns, lines, coins, frowns, meals, kills, fails, tells, dolls, goals, gulls, pulls, fools, hurls, miles, fowls.

182: Final [gz] and [ŋz]

leagues, pigs, begs, rags, hogs, morgues, rogues, hugs, fugues, ergs, brings, flings, things, stings, bangs, fangs, clangs, hangs, throngs, tongs, gongs, bungs, tongues, lungs.

183: Medial [z]

breezes, whizzes, raises, causes, dozes, buzzes, oozes, wheezed, fizzed, grazed, caused, dozed, buzzed, oozed, easy, dizzy, raisin, pheasant, hazard, dozen, cruiser, noisy, drowzy, lizard, buzzard, chasm, dazzle, presume, deserve, possess.

184: [z] sentences

She loathes making wreaths for the holidays.

The boys left a dozen raisins on the magazines.

The rose bushes were covered with leaves from the trees.

Mr. Hazzard bought a zither and a xylophone from his friends.

They saw zebras, buzzards, and lizards at the Zanesville zoo.

[ʃ] and [ʒ]

These sounds differ from [s] and [z] in having the tongue slightly further back in the mouth, and the upper surface stretched sideways, so that there is no groove from back to front. The upper surface of the tongue provides a broad channel for the breath, in contrast to the narrow channel used for [s] and [z]. The absolute pitch of [ʃ] is thus considerably lower than that of [s].

Practice Exercises 152 and 153 with the [s] words preceding the corresponding [ʃ] words. Practice Exercise 175 with the [z] words preceding the [ʒ] words. Then practice the following exercises.

Few minimal contrasts between [ʃ] and [ʒ] occur in English. Most of the pairs in this exercise involve other phonemic contrasts as well as the contrast between [ʃ] and [ʒ].

185: [ʃ] and [ʒ]

[ʃ]	[ʒ]	[ʃ]	[ʒ]
ruche	rouge	glacier	glazier
dilution	delusion	Asher	azure
Confucian	confusion	Aleutian	allusion
mission	vision	meshing	measure
Russian	erosion	seashore	seizure
leashes	leisure	precious	pleasure
cashes	casual	vicious	visual

186: Initial [ʃ] and [ʃr]

sheep, shin, shade, shed, shabby, shark, shot, shawl, show, shove, shook, shoot, shirk, shine, shout, shriek, shrimp, shred, shrank, shrove, shrub, shrewd, shrine, shroud.

187: Medial and final [ʃ]

leash, fish, mesh, trash, wash, brush, push, leashes, dishes, precious, passion, washes, Prussian, bushel, fished, meshed, mashed, squashed, hushed, pushed, machine, mission, nation, notion, brushing, cushion, Pershing, Isham.

188: Final and medial [ʒ]

rouge, mirage, camouflage, usual, casual, division, invasion, treasure, measure, persuasion, usury, composure, seizure, explosion, adhesion, incision, visual, collision, derision, provision, leisure, pleasure, seclusion, corrosion.

189: [ʃ] and [ʒ] sentences

The treasure hunter perished in the Aleutians.

They bought fish and shrimps for the Russian bishop.

The missionary measured the sugar into three dishes.

After the collision the glazier showed unusual composure.

He made provision for studying the erosion at his leisure.

[tʃ] and [dʒ]

Phonetically [tʃ] and [dʒ] are compound sounds known as affricates. A simple sequence of [t] and [ʃ] can be illustrated by a phrase such as *hat shop* [hæt ʃɑp]. The close blending of the two elements which constitutes the affricate can be illustrated by *hatchet* [hætʃət]. Thus [tʃ] and [dʒ] are generally regarded as unit phonemes. [tʃ] contrasts with [t], [ʃ], and [k]; [dʒ], with [d], [ʒ], and [g].

190: Initial [t] and [tʃ]

[t]	[tʃ]	[t]	[tʃ]
tease	cheese	tin	chin
tear	chair	top	chop
talk	chalk	tore	chore
toes	chose	turn	churn
time	chime	tide	chide

191: Final [ts] and [tʃ]

[ts]	[tʃ]	[ts]	[tʃ]
eats	each	its	itch
mats	match	starts	starch
blots	blotch	knots	notch
ports	porch	coats	coach
huts	hutch	pouts	pouch

192: Initial [ʃ] and [tʃ]

[ʃ]	[tʃ]	[ʃ]	[tʃ]
sheep	cheap	sheaf	chief
ship	chip	shin	chin
sheer	cheer	share	chare
shop	chop	shows	chose
shied	chide	shine	chine

193: Final [ʃ] and [tʃ]

[ʃ]	[tʃ]	[ʃ]	[tʃ]
leash	leech	dish	ditch
swish	switch	wish	witch
mass	match	lash	latch
marsh	march	wash	watch
mush	much	crush	crutch

194: Initial [k] and [tʃ]

[k]	[tʃ]	[k]	[tʃ]
keep	cheap	keys	cheese
kin	chin	kill	chill
care	chair	cane	chain
cat	chat	cart	chart
core	chore	cow	chow

195: Final and medial [k] and [tʃ]

[k]	[tʃ]	[k]	[tʃ]
peek	peach	pick	pitch
wreck	wretch	pack	patch
ark	arch	knock	notch
pork	porch	cluck	clutch
picked	pitched	packed	patched
kicking	kitchen	woodcock	woodchuck

196: Initial [tʃ]

chief, cheek, chip, chill, chase, chain, chair, chess, check, chat, chant, charm, chart, chop, chalk, chore, chose, choke, choose, chirp, church, chimes, child, choice, chowder.

197: Final [tʃ]

teach, pitch, hitch, wretch, stretch, scratch, arch, march, watch, porch, torch, coach, much, touch, perch, birch, couch, inch, bench, ranch, launch, punch, filch, squelch, gulch.

198: Medial [tʃ]

pitcher, bachelor, future, satchel, creature, hatchet, moisture, merchant, mischief, orchard, nature, question, Christian, reached, matched, bunched, teaches, inches, branches.

199: [tʃ] sentences

The catcher crouched and watched the pitcher.
They were drenched as they searched the orchard.
The merchant chose the site for the future arch.
The Chinese played chess with the charming child.
The marchers carried torches and branches to the church.
The wretched urchin painted the porch of the ranch house.

200: Initial [d] and [dʒ]

[d]	[dʒ]	[d]	[dʒ]
deer	jeer	din	gin
dig	jig	dale	jail
debt	jet	dam	jam
dot	jot	daunt	jaunt
dolt	jolt	dump	jump
dirk	jerk	dowel	jowl

201: Final [d] and [dʒ]

[d]	[dʒ]	[d]	[dʒ]
seed	siege	rid	ridge
aid	age	stayed	stage
head	hedge	bad	badge
charred	charge	lard	large
ford	forge	bud	budge
rained	range	build	bilge

202: Final [dz] and [dʒ]

[dz]	[dʒ]	[dz]	[dʒ]
seeds	siege	rids	ridge
raids	rage	aids	age
dreads	dredge	sleds	sledge
fords	forge	bards	barge
surds	surge	builds	bilge

Few minimal contrasts between [ʒ] and [dʒ] occur in English. Most of the pairs in the next exercise involve other contrasts as well as that between [ʒ] and [dʒ].

203: [ʒ] and [dʒ]

[ʒ]	[dʒ]	[ʒ]	[dʒ]
leisure	ledger	azure	agile
visual	vigil	usury	drudgery
collision	collegian	pleasure	pledges
version	virgin	measure	major
rouge	Scrooge	derision	dirigible
lesion	legion	division	religion

204: Initial [g] and [dʒ]

[g]	[dʒ]	[g]	[dʒ]
gear	jeer	guilt	jilt
gale	jail	get	jet
gag	jag	got	jot
gaunt	jaunt	gust	just
gorge	George	goose	juice

205: Final [g] and [dʒ]

[g]	[dʒ]	[g]	[dʒ]
league	liege	brig	bridge
rig	ridge	egg	edge
leg	ledge	bag	badge
bug	budge	drug	drudge
slug	sludge	erg	urge

206: Initial [tʃ] and [dʒ]

[tʃ]	[dʒ]	[tʃ]	[dʒ]
cheap	jeep	cheer	jeer
chin	gin	chill	gill
chest	jest	choke	joke
chain	Jane	charred	jarred
chump	jump	chunk	junk
chug	jug	chew	Jew

207: Final and medial [tʃ] and [dʒ]

[tʃ]	[dʒ]	[tʃ]	[dʒ]
leech	liege	rich	ridge
etch	edge	batch	badge
larch	large	perch	purge
search	surge	cinch	singe
lunch	lunge	lecher	ledger
etches	edges	searches	surges

208: Initial [dʒ]

jeer, gin, jade, jail, gem, jet, jab, jam, jar, job, jot, jaw, jaunt, joke, jolt, jump, jut, jury, juice, June, germ, journey, joy, joint, jibe, gyrate, jowl, jounce.

209: Final [dʒ]

siege, bridge, stage, hedge, badge, large, dodge, forge, gorge, grudge, huge, urge, merge, oblige, gouge, fringe, range, avenge, plunge, lounge, bilge, bulge, divulge.

210: Medial [dʒ]

ridged, pledged, dodged, urged, gouged, sieges, cages, badges, charges, gorges, obliges, fringes, avenges, sponges, bulges, agent, largest, forgery, gorgeous, budget, danger, agile, major, surgeon, cordial, educate, verdure, grandeur.

211: [dʒ] sentences

The surgeon sponged the engineer's jaw.
The geologist plunged from a dangerous ledge.
The major was obliged to rejoin his regiment.
The judge charged the jury in the forgery case.
The budget provided for bridges and a large jail.
June saw gorges and mountain ranges on her journey.

[j]

[j] is a palatal semivowel, the non-syllabic counterpart of the vowel [i]. It occurs initially and medially in English, but not finally. It occurs in such words as *yeast* [jist], *unit* [junɪt], and *onion* [ʌnjən]. The student should guard against two variations: one the omission of [j], so that *year* is confused with *ear*; the other, confusion with [dʒ], so that *year* is confused with *jeer*.

212: Vowel and [j]

vowel	[j]	vowel	[j]
east	yeast	ear	year
ail	Yale	am	yam
all	yawl	oak	yoke
oar	yore	oozed	used
earn	yearn	owl	yowl

Those who substitute [j] for [dʒ], or who use an intermediate sound for both [j] and [dʒ], should occasionally reverse the order of the columns in practicing Exercise 213.

213: [dʒ] and [j]

[dʒ]	[j]	[dʒ]	[j]
jeer	year	jet	yet
jell	yell	jam	yam
jot	yacht	jarred	yard
jaw	yaw	joke	yoke
Jew	you	jowl	yowl

214: Initial [j]

yeast, yield, year, Yale, yet, yell, yes, yellow, yam, yank, yacht, yard, yarn, yonder, yawn, yawl, yore, yoke, young, your, you, youth, yearn, yowl, used, unit, euchre, Europe.

215: [j] after initial consonants

pupil, puny, Puget, pure, beauty, bureau, mute, music, mutual, few, feud, funeral, fumes, future, view, cue, cube, cucumber, cure, human, humor, huge, humanity, humidity.

216: Medial [j]

genius, junior, companion, union, familiar, dominion, million, peculiar, onion, genial, opinion, senior, civilian, spaniel, accumulate, volume, continue, value, rebuke, accuse, review, argue, accurate, oculist, argument, ameliorate.

After [t], [d], and [n] American usage varies. *Tune* may be [tjun] or [tun]. *Due* and *dew* may be [dju] or [du], but *do* is always [du]. *New* and *knew* may be [nju] or [nu], but *noon* is always [nun]. Consider the usage in your part of the country.

217: [u] or [ju]

tune, tube, tuba, tumult, tutor, constitution, institution, due, dew, duty, dubious, duke, induce, reduce, knew, new, news, numeral, nuisance, nude, nucleus, annuity, gratuity.

218: [j] sentences

The European yacht won the race that year.
The seniors continued to argue humorously.
The youthful pupils raised yams and cucumbers.
Yesterday yellow daffodils bloomed in the yard.
The huge puma stood in full view of the civilians.
The genial companions sailed a yawl in Puget Sound.

Soft-Palate Consonants

Three consonants, [k], [g], and [ŋ], are made with the back of the tongue in contact with the soft palate. [k] and [g] are stop consonants, and the velar valve must be closed. [ŋ] is nasal, and the velar valve must be open.

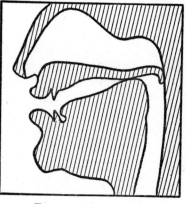

FIG. 14. [k] and [g]

The essential difference between [k] and [g] is that the vocal bands vibrate for [g] but not for [k]. A secondary difference is that English [k], at the beginning of stressed syllables, as in *clay* and *account,* is articulated with more breath pressure than [g], or than [k] in other positions, as in *skill, took,* and *taken.* Pressure of the tongue against the soft palate must therefore be increased to offset the stronger breath pressure. In Exercise 219 concentrate your attention on the voiceless quality of [k] and the voiced quality of [g], and use more tongue and breath pressure for [k].

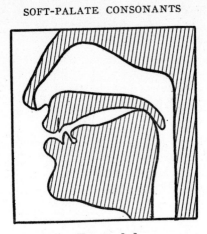

FIG. 15. [ŋ]

219: Initial [k] and [g]

[k]	[g]	[k]	[g]
kilt	guilt	came	game
cap	gap	cash	gash
card	guard	cot	got
cause	gauze	coast	ghost
come	gum	could	good
cool	ghoul	curl	girl

220: Initial [kl] and [gl], [kr] and [gr]

[k]	[g]	[k]	[g]
clean	glean	creed	greed
clays	glaze	craze	graze
clad	glad	craft	graft
clamor	glamour	crow	grow
close	glows	crew	grew
clue	glue	crime	grime

221: Final [k] and [g]

[k]	[g]	[k]	[g]
leak	league	pick	pig
peck	peg	lack	lag
back	bag	flock	flog
frock	frog	pluck	plug
broke	brogue	duck	dug
tuck	tug	irk	erg

222: Medial [k] and [g]

[k]	[g]	[k]	[g]
vicar	vigor	dicker	digger
snicker	snigger	backing	bagging
lacking	lagging	sacking	sagging
flocking	flogging	locking	logging
broken	brogan	tucking	tugging

223: Initial [t] and [k]

[t]	[k]	[t]	[k]
tease	keys	till	kill
tame	came	tamp	camp
taught	caught	tart	cart
toast	coast	took	cook
tough	cuff	tool	cool
terse	curse	tight	kite

224: Initial [st] and [sk]

[t]	[k]	[t]	[k]
steam	scheme	stiff	skiff
stale	scale	stare	scare
stamp	scamp	starves	scarves
stalled	scald	store	score
stuff	scuff	stool	school
sty	sky	stout	scout

225: [tr], [kr], [str], and [skr]

[t]	[k]	[t]	[k]
treed	creed	tripped	crypt
train	crane	tress	cress
trash	crash	trust	crust
true	crew	try	cry
stream	scream	streak	screak
strip	scrip	strap	scrap
stroll	scroll	strew	screw

226: Final [t] and [k]

[t]	[k]	[t]	[k]
cheat	cheek	sit	sick
eight	ache	debt	deck
gnat	knack	start	stark
knot	knock	taught	talk
smote	smoke	strut	struck
shirt	shirk	light	like

227: Medial [t] and [k]

[t]	[k]	[t]	[k]
knits	nicks	cheats	cheeks
eights	aches	stating	staking
knotting	knocking	slats	slacks
shirts	shirks	lighting	liking
meter	meeker	litter	liquor
lighten	liken	cattle	cackle
bitter	bicker	batter	backer
petting	pecking	patting	packing
clots	clocks	parts	parks
forts	forks	water	walker

228: Initial [p], [t], and [k]

[p]	[t]	[k]
peas	tease	keys
pin	tin	kin
pan	tan	can
post	toast	coast
puff	tough	cuff
purse	terse	curse

229: [sp], [st], and [sk]

[p]	[t]	[k]
spill	still	skill
spare	stare	scare
spanned	stand	scanned
spar	star	scar
spool	stool	school
spout	stout	scout

230: [pr], [tr], and [kr]

[p]	[t]	[k]
prick	trick	crick
prate	trait	crate
press	tress	cress
pride	tried	cried
prize	tries	cries

231: Final [p], [t], and [k]

[p]	[t]	[k]
cheap	cheat	cheek
flip	flit	flick
ape	eight	ache
slap	slat	slack
shop	shot	shock
harp	heart	hark

232: [mp], [nt], and [ŋk]

[p]	[t]	[k]
limp	lint	link
ramp	rant	rank
bump	bunt	bunk
stump	stunt	stunk
hump	hunt	hunk
camper	canter	canker

233: Initial [k]

keep, kitchen, kiss, cave, case, care, kept, cash, carve, Congo, caught, comb, coach, come, cover, could, cushion, coop, cool, curve, curse, kite, kind, coin, coil, cow, couch.

234: Initial [kr] and [skr]

crease, cringe, crate, crest, crash, crop, crawl, chrome, crust, crook, croon, crime, crouch, scream, screen, script, scribble, scrape, scrap, scratch, scrawl, scroll, screw, scribe.

235: Initial [kl]

cleat, clean, clear, cliff, clay, claim, cleft, cleanse, clap, clash, clod, clock, claw, cloth, clove, clothe, clumsy, clutch, clue, clerk, clergy, climb, cloister, cloud, clown.

236: Final [k]

leak, brick, snake, check, track, knock, talk, soak, struck, brook, fluke, like, dark, fork, lurk, silk, elk, talc, bulk, brisk, desk, task, dusk, pink, plank, honk, trunk.

237: Final [ks]

shrieks, leaks, picks, fix, flakes, wakes, decks, checks, wax, tax, marks, knocks, box, talks, hawks, forks, corks, jokes, trucks, books, dukes, works, shirks, likes, dikes.

238: Final [kt] and [kts]

peeked, tricked, raked, connect, fact, marked, flocked, talked, soaked, joked, plucked, duct, looked, lurked, worked, liked, evicts, corrects, collects, rejects, acts, facts.

239: Final [ŋkt] and [ŋks]

blinked, clinked, winked, banked, thanked, spanked, clanked, honked, flunked, junked, clunked, lynx, sinks, winks, blanks, thanks, spanks, Bronx, honks, monks, trunks, junks.

240: Medial [k]

speaker, liquor, baker, checkers, lacquer, marker, rocker, joker, trucker, lucre, worker, pickle, speckle, tackle, sparkle, local, buckle, circle, cycle, sinker, anchor, drunkard, twinkle, ankle, uncle, record, extra, accident, accessory, Turkish.

241: [k] sentences

The captain served Bronx cocktails to the crowd.

The criminal escaped by crawling under the truck.

The cargo came down the Congo to the coast of Africa.

The company rejected the crates of defective cushions.

The actor's head ached as he walked to the night club.

By a stroke of luck the clerk caught a pike in the lake.

For [g] the back of the tongue should come in contact with the soft palate, but less vigorously than for [k], and with the vocal bands vibrating. Both [k] and [g] require the velar valve to be closed. Review Exercises 220-222 to contrast [k] and [g].

242: Initial [d] and [g]

[d]	[g]	[d]	[g]
dear	gear	dig	gig
daze	gaze	debt	get
dash	gash	dot	got
dawn	gone	dough	go
dust	gust	dull	gull
dirt	girt	died	guide

243: Initial [dr] and [gr]

[d]	[g]	[d]	[g]
drill	grill	dray	gray
drain	grain	drab	grab
draft	graft	drove	grove
drone	grown	drudge	grudge
drew	grew	droop	group

244: Final [d] and [g]

[d]	[g]	[d]	[g]
lead	league	bid	big
did	dig	led	leg
sad	sag	bad	bag
road	rogue	cod	cog
bed	beg	bud	bug
thud	thug	feud	fugue

245: Medial [d] and [g]

[d]	[g]	[d]	[g]
leads	leagues	ridding	rigging
beds	begs	roads	rogues
buds	bugs	thuds	thugs
toddle	toggle	feuds	fugues
girdle	gurgle	burden	Bergen
straddle	straggle	muddy	muggy

246: Initial [b], [d], and [g]

[b]	[d]	[g]
big	dig	gig
bait	date	gate
bet	debt	get
bold	doled	gold
bust	dust	gust
berth	dearth	girth

247: Final [b], [d], and [g]

[b]	[d]	[g]
bib	bid	big
rib	rid	rig
cob	cod	cog
hob	hod	hog
robe	road	rogue

248: Initial [g]

geese, gear, gingham, gaze, guest, gather, guard, got, gong, gauze, ghost, gust, good, goose, girth, guide, goiter, gouge.

249: Initial [gr]

green, grill, grape, great, grand, grass, grotto, grove, gross, gruff, grunt, grew, groom, grime, grind, groin, ground.

250: Initial [gl]

gleam, glean, glimpse, glint, glade, glaze, glen, glare, glad, glass, gloss, glory, globe, gloat, glum, gloom, glide, glower.

251: Final [g]

league, big, twig, vague, beg, leg, flag, drag, crag, bog, fog, frog, dog, morgue, vogue, rogue, shrug, jug, fugue, erg.

252: Final [gz]

leagues, pigs, figs, digs, pegs, kegs, bags, rags, crags, fogs, hogs, dogs, morgues, rogues, plugs, rugs, fugues, ergs.

253: Final [gd]

leagued, rigged, pegged, begged, bagged, flagged, tagged, dragged, lagged, flogged, logged, jogged, plugged, drugged.

254: Medial [g]

eager, beagle, vigor, signal, vaguely, beggar, legacy, laggard, shaggy, bargain, cargo, toggle, soggy, auger, dogie, roguish, dugout, struggle, bugle, frugal, burglar, gargoyle.

255: [g] sentences

Green grapes grow in the big garden.

The shaggy dog eagerly grabbed the burglar.

The guide looked for grouse in the tall grass.

The haggard gambler was disguised as a beggar.

The guests made vague guesses about the legacy.

Grandfather gave a pet goose to the group of girls.

[ŋ]

The phoneme [ŋ] combines the tongue position of [k] and [g] with the soft-palate position of [m] and [n]. It is, in short, a soft-palate nasal, as shown in the diagram at the beginning of this section. English [ŋ] is limited to certain positions in the word and syllable. It does not occur at the beginning of any word or syllable. It occurs at the end of words, as in *sing* [sɪŋ], and of syllables, as in *singer* [sɪŋɚ]; and in the final combinations [ŋk] as in *link* [lɪŋk], [ŋks], as in *lynx* [lɪŋk], [ŋθ] as in *length* [lɛŋθ], [ŋθs] as in *lengths* [lɛŋθs], [ŋd] as in *banged* [bæŋd], and [ŋz] as in *bangs* [bæŋz].

English [ŋ] does not occur before final [g]. Such a use ordinarily indicates that the native language of the speaker is one of those in which [ŋ] is not an independent phoneme but the nasal variety used only before [k] or [g]. In English [ŋ] occurs before [g] only in the middle of such root words as *hunger* [hʌŋgɚ] and *single* [sɪŋgəl], never in such words as *hung* and *sing*. Nor does it occur as a linking sound before a following vowel, as in the phrases *hung up* and *sing out*.

Minimal contrasts exist between [m], [n], and [ŋ], as in some [sʌm], *sun* [sʌn], and *sung* [sʌŋ]; and between [g] and [ŋ], as in *bag* [bæg] and *bang* [bæŋ]. Although minimal contrasts between [ŋg] and [ŋ] do not occur, contrasts approaching the minimal do occur, and constitute useful practice material for those speakers who confuse medial [ŋg] and [ŋ].

In practicing the contrast between [ŋg] to [ŋ], you should concentrate your attention on the feeling of muscular tension in the back of your mouth. As the soft-palate valve closes in the transition from [ŋ] to [g] you should feel the increased muscular tension. On the other hand, when [ŋ] is not to be followed by [g], there should be no increase in tension. When proceeding from [ŋ] to a following vowel, be sure that there is not the slightest interruption of the flow of breath at the point of transition.

256: [ŋg] and [ŋ]

[ŋg]	[ŋ]	[ŋg]	[ŋ]
single	singer	tingle	wringer
finger	bringer	distinguish	stinger
anger	hanger	bangle	banging
languor	clanging	longer	longing
younger	youngster	stronger	strongly
hungry	tonguetied	England	singsong

In contrasting [g] and [ŋ], note that the [g] words end with an abrupt stoppage of the breath. On the other hand, the final [ŋ] should be allowed to die away gradually, even at the risk of some exaggeration in the early practice periods.

257: [g] and [ŋ]

[g]	[ŋ]	[g]	[ŋ]
brig	bring	wig	wing
rig	ring	swig	swing
bag	bang	tag	tang
rag	rang	sag	sang
gag	gang	hag	hang
bug	bung	tug	tongue
lug	lung	rug	rung

In contrasting [n] and [ŋ] the only difference should be in the placement of the tongue: the tip on the gum ridge for [n], the back on the soft palate for [ŋ]. There should be no abrupt stoppage of the breath for either [n] or [ŋ]; in your first practicing make them a little longer than seems necessary.

258: [n] and [ŋ]

[n]	[ŋ]	[n]	[ŋ]
thin	thing	sin	sing
pan	pang	ban	bang
lawn	long	gone	gong
ton	tongue	run	rung
sins	sings	wins	wings
pans	pangs	clans	clangs
lawns	longs	tons	tongues
winning	winging	banning	banging
sinner	singer	banner	banger
wind	winged	lawned	longed
fanned	fanged	band	banged

Similarly with [m], [n], and [ŋ], there should be no abrupt stoppage of the breath to suggest [mb], [nd], or [ŋg].

259: [m], [n], and [ŋ]

[m]	[n]	[ŋ]
ram	ran	rang
clam	clan	clang
rum	run	rung
some	son	sung
clams	clans	clangs
rums	runs	rungs
simmer	sinner	singer

In practicing [ŋg], be sure you do not neglect [g]; make it strong and vigorous.

260: [ŋg]

England, English, mingle, tingle, linger, single, shingle, jingle, distinguish, extinguish, angle, anger, bangle, mangle, tangle, dangle, languor, languish, wrangle, jangle, Sangamon, kangaroo, Congo, longer, longest, stronger, strongest, bungle, jungle, fungus, hunger, younger, youngest.

261: Final and medial [ŋk]

ink, blink, pink, drink, sink, wink, plank, bank, blank, frank, drank, shank, honk, hunk, trunk, sunk, slunk, shrunk, junk, blinker, trinket, twinkle, banker, banquet, thankful, bronco, conquer, donkey, monkey, flunky, drunken, sunken.

262: [ŋks] and [ŋkt]

inks, blinks, thinks, lynx, sinks, winks, shrinks, clinks, planks, pranks, banks, blanks, Manx, flanks, tanks, ranks, hanks, Bronx, honks, hunks, monks, trunks, chunks, junks, inked, blinked, linked, winked, chinked, clinked, succinct, planked, flanked, banked, ranked, spanked, honked, junked.

For final and medial [ŋ] practice slowly and in as relaxed a manner as you can. In your first practice sessions prolong [ŋ] slightly and make sure that you don't tighten the muscles in the back of the mouth at the end of the sound.

263: Final [ŋ]

bring, fling, wing, thing, ring, sing, swing, sting, sling, king, pang, bang, fang, tang, rang, sang, slang, gang, hang, long, wrong, song, strong, gong, bung, flung, tongue, lung, young, rung, sung, swung, slung, strung, hung.

264: Medial [ŋ]

bringing, flinging, winging, ringing, singer, singing, swinging, stinger, stinging, kingly, gingham, banging, hanger, anxiety, longing, wronging, length, lengths, strength, strengthen, Springfield, singsong, wingless, Binghamton, hangnail, Shanghai, Washington, songbird, songster, longhorn, tonguetied, youngster, Youngstown, Birmingham, Burlington.

265: [ŋz] and [ŋd]

brings, flings, wings, things, rings, sings, swings, slings, kings, pangs, bangs, fangs, tangs, gangs, hangs, longs, wrongs, songs, gongs, bungs, tongues, lungs, rungs, winged, banged, ganged, clanged, hanged, longed, wronged

266: [ŋg] and [ŋk] sentences

He was too hungry to wait any longer.

Mr. Ingram left England for the Congo.

He brought a pet monkey to the banquet.

The banker saw a kangaroo at the Bronx zoo.

Abraham Lincoln once lived in Sangamon County.

The youngest boy was stronger than his angry brother.

He was lost in a tangle of tree trunks in the jungle.

As the sun sank the angler was overcome with languor.

He distinguished a bit of fungus dangling from the shingles.

267: [ŋ] sentences

The red winged blackbird swung on a reed.

The strong man longed to eat a sizzling steak.

Mr. King had an exporting business in Shanghai.

The panting dog's long tongue hung from its mouth.

The songbirds came early to Youngstown this spring.

At the sound of the gong a muttering throng gathered.

The Birmingham church bells were ringing this morning.

The length and strength of the building block seemed adequate.

268: [ŋ], [ŋg], and [ŋk] sentences

The hungry donkey drank at the spring.

He hung his hat on a hook in the waiting room.

She rang a tinkling bell for the serving woman.

The kingfisher was diving into the bubbling stream.

The shingles on the building were warping in the sun.

The drunkard was doing many silly things at the banquet.

The angry woman threw the bangle across the dining room.

The spies were hiding among the bushes along the river bank.

Springfield, Burlington, and Lexington are in New England.

The longer the youngster angled, the greater grew his anguish.

The Consonant [h]

English [h] has no characteristic position of the tongue or lips, but adapts itself to the tongue or lip position of whatever sound immediately follows it. [h] consists of a puff of breath which is usually accompanied by enough contraction within the larynx to produce audible friction. The sound is limited in occurrence: it is used chiefly at the beginning of stressed syllables before vowels, and by some speakers also before [j] as in *huge* [hjudʒ] and [w] as in *whale* [hwel]. It does not occur before consonants or at the end of syllables. In medial unstressed syllables it is usually omitted, as in *shepherd* [ʃepɚd], *annihilate* [ənaɪəlet], and *inhibition* [ɪnɪbɪʃən]. To pronounce [h] in these medial unstressed syllables often gives an artificial flavor to the pronunciation.

[h] is sometimes confused, especially by foreigners, with [f], [k], and [ʍ] (or with its free variant [hw]).

269: [f] and [h]

[f]	[h]	[f]	[h]
feed	heed	fizz	his
phase	haze	fact	hacked
farm	harm	folly	holly
fed	head	fall	hall
furl	hurl	foes	hose
fight	height	fowl	howl
fill	hill	fail	hail
fence	hence	foal	whole
fold	hold	fad	had
fire	hire	foam	home

270: [k] and [h]

[k]	[h]	[k]	[h]
keep	heap	kill	hill
care	hair	catch	hatch
card	hard	cot	hot
call	hall	coast	host
could	hood	curse	hearse
kite	height	cow	how

271: [ʍ] and [h]

[ʍ]	[h]	[ʍ]	[h]
wheel	heel	wheat	heat
which	hitch	whale	hail
where	hair	when	hen
whack	hack	what	hot
whirr	her	whirl	hurl
white	height	why	high

272: Initial [h]

heap, heave, hero, hymn, hickory, hate, haze, hair, heavy, health, habit, hash, harm, hearth, hobby, hot, honk, haughty, hall, whole, hose, huddle, hung, hook, hood, hoop, whose, hurt, heard, high, hide, hire, hoyden, hound, house, hue, human, humid, humor, huge, Hughes.

273: Initial [ʍ] or [hw]

wheat, wheel, wheeze, whim, whip, whiff, whisper, whiskey, which, whey, whale, whet, when, whelp, where, whack, what, wharf, whirr, whirl, why, white, whine, while.

274: Medial [h], [hj], and [ʍ] or [hw]

ahead, ahoy, unheeded, unhealthy, unharmed, unheard, preheat, beheaded, inhabit, prohibit, cohort, vehicular, inherit, rehearse, behave, behind, upheaval, somehow, inhale, uphold, buckwheat, cartwheel, bullwhip, somewhere, anywhere, everywhere, somewhat, meanwhile, inhuman, unhumorous.

275: [h], [hj], and [ʍ] or [hw] sentences

He felt the heat in his feet and head.

They killed the hawk on the top of the hill.

The wheat field shimmered in the intense heat.

The child wailed as the whale spouted by the ship.

The sheepherder herded his longhorns on horseback.

He inhaled and exhaled slowly to see if his ribs hurt.

Buckwheat was in bloom everywhere in the hundred acres.

The law prohibits vehicular traffic anywhere in the park.

On a sudden whim he called an extra rehearsal in the hall.

Part III

VOWELS AND DIPHTHONGS

English Vowels

The vowels of any language are less restricted in their range of variability than the consonants. For most consonants there is a specific contact between parts of the speaking mechanism, such as the contact between the lower lip and the upper teeth for English [f], or between the back of the tongue and the soft palate for English [k].

For vowels, however, there are no such contacts. The tongue is free in the mouth, and the relative position of the tongue, the jaw, and the lips regulates the size and shape of the mouth cavity, and the resulting vowel quality. Slight changes in these relative positions produce slight changes in vowel quality, and the possible range of vowel quality is thus a continuum with no sharp boundaries such as those which differentiate consonants.

Every language divides the vowel continuum, according to immemorial habit, into certain significant units, the vowel phonemes of that particular language. If there are few vowel phonemes, as in Tagalog or Spanish, the possible range of variation in the pronunciation of each vowel will be great. If there are more vowel phonemes, the possible range of variation which can take place without producing ambiguity is necessarily reduced.

In English there are well over a dozen vowel phonemes, the exact number depending on the regional type. In comparison with the five vowel phonemes of Spanish or Japanese, or the seven of Italian, this large number necessarily imposes a limit on the range which any English vowel may have without producing ambiguity. English must distinguish, for instance, between *seat*

99

and *sit,* a distinction which does not need to be made in Spanish or Italian.

To differentiate vowel phonemes, English makes use of four physical factors: (1) the tongue and jaw may be higher or lower; the vowel of *sit* occupies a high position, that of *set* a mid-high position, and that of *sat* a low position. (2) The tongue may be arched further forward or backward in the mouth, as in *baste* with the arch in front, *burst* with the arch in the center, and *boast* with the arch in back. (3) The upper surface of the tongue may be made convex from side to side by muscular tension, or left relatively flat if the muscles remain relaxed.

This muscular tension can be felt by the fingers through the loose skin under the jaw and directly behind the chin. Thus *peel, pail,* and *pool* require tense muscles; *pill, bell,* and *pull* require lax muscles. Variable muscular tension is characteristic of only a few languages. For most foreigners it will be one of the more difficult aspects of English vowel pronunciation.

Finally (4), a certain amount of lip rounding, although not essential for all varieties of English, is usually desirable for easy understanding. Thus the vowels of *pool, pole, pull,* and *Paul* ordinarily involve some rounding of the lips, *pool* most, *Paul* least.

Because of the multiplicity of English vowel phonemes, the skill most important to acquire is that of making unambiguous contrasts between them. A large share of the exercises that follow involve practice in making such contrasts. The foreigner, in particular, should practice the contrasts before attempting to achieve relative uniformity for any single vowel phoneme.

Front Vowels

[i] and [ɪ]

Both [i] and [ɪ] are formed with the tongue arched high in the front of the mouth. The phoneme [i] is familiar to speakers of most languages, but a foreign flavor may persist if the foreign speaker regards it as identical with his native [i]. Whenever English [i] is prolonged it is characterized by a gradually increasing muscular tension which can be symbolized by [ɪi]. Thus English *see* [sɪi] is by no means identical with French or Spanish *si* [si] because of the gliding quality of the native English sound. On the other hand, [ɪ] remains lax throughout its duration, and this lax utterance may be completely unfamiliar to the foreigner. In beginning your practicing, put your fingers under your jaw, and try to feel the increasing muscular bulge which indicates tongue tension for [ɪi], and at the same time try to avoid any such tension for [ɪ].

276: [ɪi] and [ɪ]

[ɪi]	[ɪ]	[ɪi]	[ɪ]
eat	it	each	itch
deep	dip	sheep	ship
beet	bit	scheme	skim
peach	pitch	reed	rid
feast	fist	scene	sin
peak	pick	steel	still
deem	dim	feel	fill
greet	grit	heap	hip
neat	knit	leak	lick

277: Initial and final [ɪi]

even, ether, Edith, east, easy, equal, eager, eating, evil, Easter, eagle, eaves, plea, bee, free, three, tea, tree, see, she, key, agree, he, spree, glee, knee, ski, we.

278: Medial [ɪi]

peel, beet, breed, meal, feet, veal, team, deep, niece, leash, cheese, heat, people, Cæsar, Stephen, steeple, stream, please, preach, greedy, machine, police, achieve, careen.

279: Initial [ɪ]

imp, inch, ill, itch, idiom, igloo, ignorant, Indian, image, idiot, imitate, implement, incident, ink, index, Isabel, inland, issue, isthmus, Italy, ear, Erie, irritate.

280: Medial [ɪ]

pink, pig, busy, build, milk, thing, thick, width, whiskers, still, trip, dig, drink, single, ship, shrink, chicken, ring, kiss, give, spirit, mirror, steer, serious, fierce, miracle.

281: [ɪi] and [ɪ] sentences

Italy is not an isthmus but a peninsula.
Wilbur wrote his initials in indelible ink.
Steel mills have made Pittsburgh a rich city.
Edith and Isabel grew sweet peas on a trellis.
The automobile nearly skidded into the deep ditch.
The greeting card industry is bigger than it used to be.

Stephen is studying the history of the East India Company.

Virginia spent three weeks before Christmas at Miami Beach.

[e] and [ɛ]

These vowels bear the same essential relationship to each other as [i] and [ɪ], but with the jaw and tongue lowered to the mid position. [e] is mid high, front, and tense; [ɛ] is mid high, front and lax. When [e] is prolonged it develops an important glide form which may be represented by [eɪ]; this, rather than a pure [e], is the form the foreigner should try to acquire.

282: [ɪi] and [eɪ]

[ɪi]	[eɪ]	[ɪi]	[eɪ]
sheep	shape	seem	same
chief	chafe	sleeve	slave
meet	mate	feast	faced
feed	fade	scene	sane
feel	fail	weak	wake
lease	lace	tree	tray

In contrasting [ɪ] and [ɛ] avoid all muscular tension; the only difference is that [ɪ] has a high position of the tongue and jaw; [ɛ], a mid high position.

283: [ɪ] and [ɛ]

[ɪ]	[ɛ]	[ɪ]	[ɛ]
itch	etch	lift	left
slipped	slept	wrist	rest
rich	wretch	did	dead
built	belt	tin	ten
fill	fell	cheer	chair
sneer	snare	big	beg

In contrasting [e] and [ɛ], remember muscular tension and a gliding turning [e] into [eɪ], and no muscular tension for [ɛ]. Both [eɪ] and [ɛ] require the jaw and tongue to be mid high.

284: [eɪ] and [ɛ]

[eɪ]	[ɛ]	[eɪ]	[ɛ]
age	edge	bait	bet
paste	pest	sprayed	spread
wage	wedge	main	men
fail	fell	rake	wreck
lace	less	sail	sell
weight	wet	spatial	special

285: Initial [eɪ]

ape, apron, April, able, aim, aphid, atheist, eighty, aid, age, ail, ace, Asia, ache, ague, aviator, amiable, aimless.

286: Final [eɪ]

pay, pray, play, bay, may, they, tray, day, neigh, lay, say, stay, spray, gay, ray, hay, away, betray, display, delay.

287: Medial [eɪ]

grape, baby, shame, wave, freight, grade, train, pale, space, graze, wage, rake, vague, bacon, vacant, major, naked.

288: Initial [ɛ]

edge, extra, empty, end, egg, elbow, Edward, Essex, effort, educate, elevate, estimate, ever, excellent, emperor, epic, Ezra.

289: Medial [ε]

pet, best, mend, fell, then, tempt, dead, next, left, sent, wrench, kept, guess, step, steady, jealous, breakfast, deceptive.

290: [eɪ] and [ε] sentences

A pin and a pen lay on a plate on the desk.
Elsa helped herself to the peppermint sticks.
Many evergreen trees shaded the village lanes.
Many men donated blood at the Red Cross center.
They relished the flavor of the excellent grapes.
The street went straight to the railroad station.
Edward and Ezra took the elevator to the eighth floor.
Her visit to the Philadelphia mint meant a great deal to Ethel.

The low front vowel [æ]

For [æ] the tongue and jaw must be low, and the tongue must be kept well forward in the mouth. Usually the tongue muscles are lax, and should never become more than slightly tense. Remember that [ε] requires a higher tongue position, and that [eɪ] requires both a higher tongue and greater tension.

291: [ε] and [æ]

[ε]	[æ]	[ε]	[æ]
pet	pat	gem	jam
lend	land	said	sad
shell	shall	wren	ran
beg	bag	flesh	flash
neck	knack	slept	slapped
kept	capped	temper	tamper

292: [eɪ] and [æ]

[eɪ]	[æ]	[eɪ]	[æ]
cape	cap	hate	hat
fate	fat	main	man
maid	mad	shale	shall
cane	can	wakes	wax
James	jams	shame	sham
faked	fact	aches	ax

Practice the high, mid, and low front vowel positions.

293: [ɪ], [ɛ], and [æ]

[ɪ]	[ɛ]	[æ]
him	hem	ham
sit	set	sat
hid	head	had
pick	peck	pack
big	beg	bag
slipped	slept	slapped

294: Initial [æ]

apple, abbey, amble, avarice, Athens, atom, add, annual, Alice, ashes, accident, accurate, agony, adjutant, allocate, angry, anchor, alcohol, analyze, Africa, aggravate, Amsterdam.

295: Medial [æ]

pack, bank, bag, mad, fat, fancy, vat, thank, than, tack, damp, knack, lamb, rag, sack, shack, chat, jam, yank, cap, gap, hand, manifest, tanker, satisfy, banish, balance, California.

296: [æ] sentences

The beggar carried a big black bag on his back.

Ashes, sand, and wax were scattered in the pan.

She had the knack of making batter for pancakes.

He balanced a platter of sandwiches on his hand.

Alice traveled to Athens and Africa on a tanker.

The ambulance used ten gallons of gasoline that day.

The ambassador thanked my grandmother for the apple.

The actress bought a fancy handkerchief in California.

Back Vowels

The low back vowel [ɑ]

This vowel differs from [æ] in having the tongue well back in the mouth, in contrast to the forward position for [æ]. Like [æ], however, it is made with lax muscles and unrounded lips. In Exercise 297 concentrate your attention on this forward and backward movement of the tongue.

297: [æ] and [ɑ]

[æ]	[ɑ]	[æ]	[ɑ]
am	arm	at	art
cap	carp	patch	parch
lad	lard	had	hard
badge	barge	ban	barn
mash	marsh	hash	harsh
lack	lark	shack	shark

Most Americans pronounce the words with *o*-spellings in Exercise 298 with [ɑ]. Some Americans use [ɒ], a variation with slight lip-rounding which will be discussed in Exercise 308. Foreigners will be most readily understood if they aim for the unrounded vowel [ɑ].

298: [æ] and [ɑ]

[æ]	[ɑ]	[æ]	[ɑ]
ax	ox	add	odd
map	mop	jab	job
gnat	not	clad	clod
band	bond	lack	lock
backs	box	flap	flop
attar	otter	apposition	opposition

299: [ɑr]

arm, arch, ardent, argue, sharp, marble, charm, scarf, starve, farther, start, guard, barn, Charleston, harsh, marsh, starch, march, barge, margin, bark, stark, bargain, argument.

300: [ɑ]

odd, ox, otter, option, opposite, obvious, obstinate, occident, optimist, stop, crop, rob, mob, bomb, pomp, spot, shot, rod, fodder, pond, response, policy, shock, stock.

301: [ɑ] sentences

The carpenter parked his car near the marsh.

The sergeant stood guard at the bomber plant.

The barn stood beyond the pond near the garden.

The operator timed the machine with a stop watch.

The bargain basement was mobbed by ardent shoppers.

The farmers fed their garbage to the starving hogs.

The barge carried marble down the river to Charleston.

The low back vowel [ɔ]

This vowel differs from [ɑ] in two major respects. The tongue muscles must be more tense, and the lips rounded. Sometimes [ɔ] has a slightly higher tongue position than [ɑ], but this is of minor importance.

Most Americans make a clear distinction between [ɑ] and [ɔ]. Some distinguish in some categories, for instance *barn* and *born,* but not in others, such as *cot* and *caught.* Some words, like *forest* and *log,* have [ɑ] in one part of the country, [ɔ] in another. The foreigner will be most readily understood if he makes a clear distinction between [ɑ] and [ɔ] and follows regional usage with respect to words like *log* and *forest*.

In the following exercises concentrate your attention on making [ɑ] lax and unrounded, [ɔ] tense and rounded. Keep your tongue well back in your mouth for both sounds.

302: [ɑr] and [ɔr]

[ɑ]	[ɔ]	[ɑ]	[ɔ]
are	or	far	for
part	port	barn	born
farm	form	card	cord
parch	porch	park	pork
lard	lord	martyr	mortar
farce	force	stark	stork

303: [ɑ] and [ɔ]

[ɑ]	[ɔ]	[ɑ]	[ɔ]
odd	awed	ox	auks
knot	naught	rot	wrought
cot	caught	hock	hawk
nod	gnawed	sod	sawed
clod	clawed	collar	caller
box	balks	chock	chalk

304: [ɔr]

or, order, orbit, organ, orchid, orchard, orphan, porch, border, morning, morbid, form, vortex, thorn, torn, dormer, north, lord, sword, short, corn, Gordon, horse.

305: [ɔ]

awe, author, awning, alter, awkward, August, Paul, ball, malt, false, tall, dawn, naught, lawn, raw, sought, shawl, chalk, yawn, caught, gauze, hawk.

306: [ɔ] sentences

The autoist bought a box of calking compound.

The awkward dwarf brandished a sword for sport.

His daughter marked up the sidewalk with chalk.

The lawyer called to the short auctioneer.

Paul and Norman saw the New York Yankees play ball.

The author turned at the corner and snorted with scorn.

The horse's halter was caught on a thorn tree in the orchard.

Variable Low Vowels

The vowels [a] and [ɒ] are used by some Americans, but not by all. Some understanding of them is desirable, even though you yourself may not need or wish to use them.

The vowel [a] is low and lax, and the tongue placement is intermediate, not so far forward as [æ], not so far back as [ɑ]. To the ear it seems intermediate between [æ] and [ɑ]. It is used chiefly in two types of words. In eastern New England it is used in words like *far, farm,* and *father,* which are there often pronounced as [faː], [faːm], and [faːðə].

It is also used in a group of words illustrated by exercise 307 in eastern New England and eastern Virginia, where, however, its use has been declining in favor of [æ]. Elsewhere in the United States, [a] occurs only sporadically and inconsistently, generally under elocutionary influence.

The dictionary practice of using separate diacritic markings to identify words of the class of *ask, dance,* and *path,* and to differentiate them from *bad, grand, thanks,* and *fancy,* is merely a device to indicate that the first group of words is variable in pronunciation, the second relatively fixed. You should not interpret the difference in diacritics as a mandate for you to pronounce *ask* and *ax* with different vowels. Here, as always, you should be guided by the general educated usage of your part of the country.

307: [æ], [a], or [ɑ]

advance, advantage, after, answer, ask, aunt, basket, bath, blanch, blast, branch, brass, calf, calves, can't, cask, casket, cast, caste, castle, castor, chaff, chance, chant, clasp, class, command, craft, dance, demand, draft, draught, enchant, example, fast, fasten, flask, France, Frances, Francis, gasp, glance, glass, graft, grant, grass, half, halves, hasp, lance, last, lath, laugh, mask, mast, master, nasty, pass, past, pastor, pasture, path, plant, plaster, prance, raft, rafter, rasp, sample, shaft, slant, staff, task, trance, vast.

The vowel [ɒ] is low and lax, like [ɑ], but has slight lip rounding, like [ɔ]. It sounds intermediate between [ɑ] and [ɔ]. The vowels [ɑ], [ɒ], and [ɔ] form highly complex patterns in American English, and their use differs markedly in different parts of the country.

The vowel [ɒ] occurs most frequently in eastern New England, in western Pennsylvania, and in scattered areas of the West. In these areas we are often compelled to depend on context for the interpretation of such pairs as *cot* and *caught, stock* and *stalk,* and *rot* and *wrought,* since either [ɑ], [ɒ], or [ɔ] may be used in any of them. The foreigner should, of course, make a clear distinction between *cot* [kɑt] and *caught* [kɔt] and similar pairs, simply on the ground that his speech is more likely to produce ambiguity than that of the native, and that he should utilize every opportunity to be understood easily.

One of the important uses of [ɒ] is as a variant of [ɔ] before the consonants [f], [θ], and [s], in such words as *cough, cloth,* and *cross.* Dictionaries sometimes use separate diacritic markings for such words, in order to keep the categories straight, not, however, to lay down any mandate for the use of [ɒ]. Exercise 308 illustrates the category.

308: [ɔ] or [ɒ]

offer, office, often, doff, cough, scoff, trough, broth, moth, froth, boss, Boston, moss, toss, dross, Ross, floss, frost, loss, lost, loft, oft, coffee, cross, coffin, cost, gloss, foster.

Certain words permit a variation ranging all the way from [ɑ], through [ɒ], to [ɔ], usually with a regional preference. Thus [ɑ] predominates along the Atlantic and Gulf coasts in words in which the vowel is followed by [r] and another vowel, as in *forest, orange, horrid,* and *coral*. Further west, [ɔ] predominates in the same words. In words in which [g] follows the vowel, as in *log, fog,* and *frog,* the same range from [ɑ], through [ɒ], to [ɔ] occurs, but the regional predominance is more complex, and less clear.

309: [ɑ], [ɒ], or [ɔ]

orange, oracle, orator, porridge, borrow, morrow, moral, forest, foreign, torrent, torrid, Doris, Dorothy, Laura, Lawrence, sorrow, sorry, coral, coroner, coronation, quarrel, quarantine, quarry, warrant, bog, fog, flog, frog, dog, log, soggy, cog, clog, hog.

[ʌ]

[ʌ] is a back lax vowel with the tongue raised mid high; it thus bears the same relationship to [ɑ] as [ɛ] to [æ]. Some Americans place the tongue slightly further forward; most keep it well back. In Exercise 310 the tongue should be consistently higher for [ʌ] than for [ɑ].

310: [ɑ] and [ʌ]

[ɑ]	[ʌ]	[ɑ]	[ʌ]
rob	rub	cop	cup
pomp	pump	rot	rut
fond	fund	sodden	sudden
wan	won	wander	wonder
dock	duck	lock	luck
stock	stuck	clock	cluck

In contrasting [ʌ] and [ɔ], the lips must be kept rounded and the tongue muscles somewhat tense for [ɔ]. But the lips must be unrounded, the tongue muscles relaxed, and the tongue raised to the mid position for [ʌ].

311: [ɔ] and [ʌ]

[ɔ]	[ʌ]	[ɔ]	[ʌ]
bought	but	bauble	bubble
caught	cut	caller	color
hall	hull	pawn	pun
fawn	fun	dawn	done
balk	buck	talk	tuck
stalk	stuck	chalk	chuck

312: [ʌ]

upper, oven, other, under, onion, usher, ugly, cup, some, lump, mother, shut, flood, puff, love, shovel, fund, tunnel, gull, fuss, buzz, crush, much, stuck, rug, lung, shrunk, lunge.

313: [ʌ] sentences

The monkey hid under the oven till dusk.
My brother won a loving cup for the broad jump.
My uncle had huckleberries and honey for lunch.

The usher touched the ugly umbrella with disgust.

Mother had company in the front room of the bungalow.

My cousin shoveled a tunnel into the hulking mountain.

[o]

The vowel [o] is mid high, tense, and rounded. It occupies the same essential position in the back series as [e] in the front. It is in much the same position as [ʌ], but has tense muscles and rounded lips, where [ʌ] does not. It is higher in the back of the mouth than [ɔ]. Like [e], one of its principal varieties involves a slight rise in the position of the tongue when the sound is prolonged, a variation which may be symbolized by [oʊ]. It is this diphthongal variation at which the foreigner should aim.

314: [ʌ] and [oʊ]

[ʌ]	[oʊ]	[ʌ]	[oʊ]
sup	soap	come	comb
nut	note	glut	gloat
must	most	mud	mode
cult	colt	stun	stone
fuzz	foes	hull	whole
suck	soak	pucker	poker

315: [ɔ] and [oʊ]

[ɔ]	[oʊ]	[ɔ]	[oʊ]
awe	owe	auk	oak
bought	boat	scald	scold
lawn	loan	ball	bowl
pause	pose	gauze	goes
stalk	stoke	chalk	choke
flaw	flow	gnaw	know

In contrasting [e] and [o] concentrate your attention on the forward movement of the tongue for [e], and the backward movement for [o]. The foreigner should aim for the diphthongal variations [eɪ] and [oʊ].

316: [eɪ] and [oʊ]

[eɪ]	[oʊ]	[eɪ]	[oʊ]
lay	low	tame	tome
ache	oak	gate	goat
grape	grope	made	mode
pail	pole	drain	drone
raced	roast	raise	rose
wake	woke	vague	vogue

317: [oʊ]

open, over, odor, oak, rope, robe, loaf, stove, both, boat, boast, bolt, road, rolled, groan, rolls, dose, doze, soak, vogue, blow, though, toe, dough, know, low, sew, crow, glow, hoe, woe.

318: [oʊ] sentences

The couple eloped in a motor boat.
He traveled slowly from Ohio to Oklahoma.
Mr. Hogan boasted about his old oak trees.
The road led over rolling hills to the ocean.
The goat was going slowly through the oat field.
Mrs. Jones dozed by the stove as she tried to sew.

The Vowels [u] and [ʊ]

These two vowels are made with the tongue high in the back of the mouth. [u] requires tense muscles for both tongue and lips, and the lips should be well rounded. When the vowel is prolonged the tension increases, producing a diphthongal variation which may be symbolized by [ʊu]. The diphthongal form parallels the forms [ɪi], [eɪ], and [oʊ] and is the form to be aimed at by the foreigner.

The vowel [ʊ] requires lax tongue and lip muscles, and the lip rounding is less vigorous than for [u], though it should be present. A few comparisons will help to place these vowels more accurately.

In comparison with [o], which is mid high, back, tense, and rounded, [u] requires a higher tongue position and more vigorous lip rounding. In comparison with [i], which is high, front, and tense, [u] requires the tongue to be retracted into the back position, with vigorous lip rounding.

In comparison with [ʌ], which is mid high, back, and lax, [ʊ] requires a higher tongue position, and lip rounding. In comparison with [ɪ], which is high, front, and lax, [ʊ] requires the tongue to be retracted into the back position, with lip rounding. Try to feel these differences in the adjustment of tongue and lips as you practice.

319: [oʊ] and [ʊu]

[oʊ]	[ʊu]	[oʊ]	[ʊu]
owes	ooze	moan	moon
soap	soup	boat	boot
pole	pool	roam	room
grove	groove	boast	boost
roast	roost	coal	cool
toe	too	show	shoe

320: [ɪi] and [ʊu]

[ɪi]	[ʊu]	[ɪi]	[ʊu]
ease	ooze	mean	moon
sweep	swoop	beet	boot
peel	pool	ream	room
grieve	groove	beast	boost
bean	boon	keel	cool
tea	too	she	shoe

321: [ʌ] and [ʊ]

[ʌ]	[ʊ]	[ʌ]	[ʊ]
buck	book	tuck	took
luck	look	ruck	rook
shuck	shook	cud	could
stud	stood	putt	put

322: [ɪ] and [ʊ]

[ɪ]	[ʊ]	[ɪ]	[ʊ]
hid	hood	fill	full
pill	pull	kid	could
fit	foot	will	wool
peer	poor	sheer	sure
beer	boor	mere	moor

323: [ʊu] and [ʊ]

[ʊu]	[ʊ]	[ʊu]	[ʊ]
pool	pull	fool	full
Luke	look	cooed	could
wooed	wood	who'd	hood
boom	book	room	rook
tomb	took	food	good

324: [ʊu]

ooze, too, do, shoe, woo, who, through, loop, soup, room, whom, groove, booth, boot, hoot, boost, roost, mood, food, tool, cool, soon, spoon, loose, moose, snooze, choose, rouge.

Before *r,* spellings may suggest [ʊu] when the sound is actually [ʊ]; always use [ʊ] before *r* in monosyllables.

325: [ʊ]

put, pull, push, pudding, book, bush, bull, bushel, bullet, bulletin, foot, full, took, look, rook, shook, could, stood, good, cook, hook, poor, boor, moor, sure, tour, tourist, assure, jury.

326: [ʊu] and [ʊ] sentences

Put the books on the stool in the back room.
He put his foot in the boot and pulled it on.
He pushed the food away from him with a spoon.
The tourist saw the moon shining on the brook.
The bullet left a groove on the bulletin board.
The moose stood on the moor looking for food.

The combination [ju] is often disguised by the spelling. It is easily recognizable in *you, youth,* and *Yule,* less easily recognizable in *ewe, few, view, beauty,* and *feud.* Most often, however, its spelling is a single *u,* as in *unit, music, funeral, cube,* and *huge,* in which the single letter obscures the double nature of the sound sequence. As in other combinations, the [u] in [ju] builds up its tension gradually; an important variation, for which the foreigner should aim, is [jʊu].

327: [ʊu] and [jʊu]

[ʊu]	[jʊu]	[ʊu]	[jʊu]
oozed	used	coo	cue
who	hue	moot	mute
booty	beauty	coot	cute
food	feud	fool	fuel
moos	muse	whose	hews

328: [juu]

use, unit, union, uniform, unify, unity, universe, usual, usury, usurp, Utah, utilize, pew, pewter, puny, beauty, few, funeral, future, fuse, view, mew, music, mute, mutiny, cue, cube, cute, accuse, hue, huge, human, humor, humid.

Before *r*, spellings may suggest [juu] when the sound is actually [ju]; always use [ju] before *r* in monosyllables.

329: [ju]

pure, purity, mural, immure, fury, furious, curate, curative, curator, secure, curious, procure, spurious, impure, bureau.

Variable forms

After [r] and [l], an earlier pronunciation with [ju] has largely been superseded by a pronunciation with [u] in such words as *rude, prude, prune, brew, frugal, true, Truman, truth, shrewd, shrew, crew, cruel, crude, grew, luminous, lunatic, lucid, lute, Pluto, blue, blew, flue, flew, flute, fluke, slew, sluice, clue,* and *glue.* Nothing is to be gained by restoring the older [ju].

A few speakers, mostly radio and TV announcers, continue to use [ju] after [s] and [z], as in *sue, suit, suitable, suicide, Susan, supreme, sewer, assume, consume,* and *presume,* but most Americans use [u]. Nothing is to be gained by attempting to change from [u] to [ju] in such words, and the danger of confusing *sue* and *suit* with *shoe* and *shoot* is always present in such attempts.

After [t], [d], and [n], however, there is genuine variation. In the south of England, and in the American South, [ju] occurs regularly, and [ju] before *r*. In the rest of the United States, [u] is usual, and [u] before *r*. In practicing, the important criterion is enough consistency to make your speech inconspicuous. While you are practicing, remember the [juu] and [uu] forms.

330: [ʊu] and [ʊ] or [jʊu] and [jʊ]

tube, tune, tumor, tutor, tuba, Tudor, tuition, tulip, tuna, Tuesday, tumult, tunic, stew, stupid, student, studio, studios, stupefy, constitution, institution, dew, due, dubious, duty, dune, duel, duke, durable, during, endure, new, knew, news, newt, Newton, numeral, numerous, neuter, nude, nuisance, nucleus, nutrition, Newport, Newman, inure, penurious.

Some speakers, in their attempts to acquire the [j] of Exercise 329, have gone too far, and have developed a spurious [j] in words in which it did not belong. Some of the more common intrusions of [j] before [u], [ʊ], or a weaker vowel are illustrated in Exercise 330.

331: avoid [j]

too, noon, canoe, column, percolator, escalator, do, metabolism, sterilize, stabilize, tremendous, Marguerite, similar, coupon, assimilate, dissimilate, dissimilar.

332: [jʊu] and [jʊ], [ʊu] and [ʊ] sentences

The crew of the crude sloop were cruising to Europe.

The students mutinied when the university raised tuition.

Mr. Newman argued with Mr. Gulick about his penurious ways.

He assumed that the funeral would be at two o'clock on Tuesday.

On numerous occasions he put the wrong numerals on the coupons.

The percolator boiled over as he was watching the curious tumult.

Central Vowels with [r]

The words *turn, birth, berth, learn, worst,* and *journal,* despite differences in spelling, all use the same basic vowel. Foreign vowels which approximate this English vowel most closely are those of German *hören* and French *peur,* but the English vowel places the tongue slightly further back, and lacks the lip rounding of the French and German vowels.

The English vowel is made with the tongue mid high in the central position, neither as far forward as the front vowel [e] nor as far back as the back vowel [o]. It has four principal varieties: [ɝ], a tense vowel used in monosyllables like *turn,* and in the accented syllables of longer words like *journal.* Essentially a vocalic [r], it can best be acquired by prolonging the initial American [r] of *red.* A regional variety from which the [r]-coloring has been lost is symbolized by [ɜ]. The vowels of German *schön* and French *peu* approximate [ɜ], but with the differences already noted with respect to [ɝ].

Speakers in eastern New England, in the coastal South, and some of those in New York City and nearby areas use [ɜ] without any trace of [r]-coloring; similarly they eliminate the final [r] of *fear, fair, far, for,* and *poor,* and preconsonantal [r] in such words as *farm, form,* and *feared.*

Most Americans use [ɝ] in *turn* and *journal* and [r] in *far* and *form.* The foreigner will probably be more readily understood if he follows majority American usage and uses [ɝ] and [r].

A diphthongal development of [ɜ] may sometimes be heard in New York City and parts of the coastal South, so that *turn* becomes [tɜɪn] and *worst,* [wɜɪst]. In New York City the diphthong is generally regarded as substandard, and is apparently declining in use. In the South it generally passes unnoticed.

In unstressed positions the lax vowels [ɚ] and [ə] replace [ɝ] and [ɜ]. Thus *murmur* is [mɝmɚ] for most Americans, but [mɜmə] for some in eastern New England, New York City, and the coastal South.

The vowel [ə] has two other uses: it replaces [r] in words like *fear, beard, fare, fared, sure,* and *insured* in the "[r]-less" regions already indicated. These words then become [fɪə], [bɪəd], [fɛə], [fɛəd], [ʃʊə], and [ɪnʃʊəd]. Secondly, [ə] serves in all forms of American speech as a general unstressed vowel in such words as *above* [əbʌv], *soda* [sodə], *taken* [tekən], *bacon* [bekən], *caucus* [kɔkəs], *April* [eprəl], and *gracious* [greʃəs].

Similarities of both sound and spelling often produce confusion between [ɝ] and [ɜ] and other vowels. The next exercises will give you practice in distinguishing them.

333: [ʊr] or [ɝ] contrasted with [ɝ] or [ɜ]

[ʊr]	[ɝ]	[ʊr]	[ɝ]
boor	burr	boors	burrs
moor	myrrh	poor	purr
spoor	spur	sure	shirr

334: [ɔr], [ɔə], or [ɔː] contrasted with [ɝ] or [ɜ]

[ɔr]	[ɝ]	[ɔr]	[ɝ]
or	err	for	fur
form	firm	born	burn
torn	turn	horse	hearse
port	pert	court	curt
porch	perch	course	curse

335: [ɪr] or [ɪə] contrasted with [ɝ] or [ɜ]

[ɪr]	[ɝ]	[ɪr]	[ɝ]
ear	err	fear	fur
beard	bird	steer	stir
pierce	purse	hear	her
seared	surd	speared	spurred

336: [ɛr] or [ɛə] contrasted with [ɝ] or [ɜ]

[ɛr]	[ɝ]	[ɛr]	[ɝ]
air	err	fair	fur
spare	spur	stare	stir
bear	burr	wear	were
cared	curd	hair	her
pared	purred	blared	blurred

337: [ɑr] or [ɑː] contrasted with [ɝ] or [ɜ]

[ɑr]	[ɝ]	[ɑr]	[ɝ]
far	fur	star	stir
farm	firm	carve	curve
heart	hurt	hard	heard
yarn	yearn	starling	sterling
lark	lurk	shark	shirk

338: [ʌ] contrasted with [ɝ] or [ɜ]

[ʌ]	[ɝ]	[ʌ]	[ɝ]
cub	curb	hut	hurt
tough	turf	bust	burst
such	search	gull	girl
bud	bird	luck	lurk
fun	fern	huddle	hurdle
hull	hurl	summons	sermons

339: [ɔɪ] contrasted with [ɝ] or [ɜ]

[ɔɪ]	[ɝ]	[ɔɪ]	[ɝ]
foist	first	Hoyt	hurt
foil	furl	Boyd	bird
voice	verse	loin	learn
oily	early	coil	curl
avoid	averred	adjoin	adjourn

340: [ɝ] or [ɜ]

earth, urge, early, urban, ermine, urchin, purr, blur, stir, spur, cur, her, were, turpentine, serpent, permanent, disturb, superb, termite, sermon, skirmish, surface, swerve, birth, further, worthy, myrtle, thirty, certain, merchant.

341: [ɚ] or [ə]

copper, rubber, hammer, offer, diver, ether, bother, motor, ladder, banner, color, racer, razor, pressure, measure, mirror, catcher, ledger, baker, eager, singer, rivers, brothers, wandered, treasured, lantern, mustard, orchard, wizard, Robert.

342: [ə]

appoint, about, afford, avoid, attempt, admit, annoy, allow, assist, azalea, assure, achieve, adjust, account, agree, Cuba, comma, sofa, Eva, data, soda, Vienna, Ella, plaza, Russia, Asia, era, Ithaca, toga, bacon, circus, gracious, syrup, column, forum.

343: [ɝ], [ɜ], [ɚ], and [ə] sentences

Robert heard the whirring wings of the bird.

The clerk emerged from behind a purple curtain.

The merchant and the banker consulted the ledger.

The equator is an imaginary circle around the earth.

Much urban property was permanently damaged by termites.

The surgeon furnished his office with dark-colored furniture.

Diphthongs

Although the etymology of *diphthong* indicates the meaning "two sounds," an English diphthong is actually a continuous gliding sound within the limits of a single syllable. It is characterized by movement of the speech agents rather than by position. A sequence of vowel sounds in successive syllables, as in *react* and *coerce,* represents a leap from one vowel position to another, and is consequently quite different from such true diphthongs as those in *buy, boy,* and *bough.*

Because of long established speech habits, English has acquired an instability of the speech agents for vowels which are either tense or lengthened or both. The vowels [i] in *see,* [e] in *say,* [o] in *so,* and [u] in *who* illustrate this instability. *Sea* is regularly [sɪi], the tension of the muscles increasing as the vocal sound is prolonged. In the same way, *who* is regularly [huʊ]. *Say* is regularly [seɪ] or [sɛɪ] or some other shading which would require complicated symbolization. *So* is regularly [soʊ] or some other shading.

Obviously these variations are not meaningfully significant. They do not signify the difference between one meaning and another, and the diphthongal variants are minimized when the vowels have a shorter duration, as in *seat, gate, boat,* and *hoot.* They are, however, stylistically important. The native speaker of English uses the dipthongal variants automatically. The foreigner, who is likely to have fewer diphthongal vowels in his native language, must learn to do so.

Aside from these non-distinctive diphthongs, English has three which are phonemic, that is, diphthongs which must be maintained if the meaning is not to be changed, lost, or determined only by the context. These diphthongs are [ɔɪ] in *boy* and *foil,* [ɑʊ] in *bough* and *pound,* and [aɪ] in *buy* and *life.* If *foil* [fɔɪl] loses its diphthongal glide it becomes [fɔl], or *fall.*

126

If *pound* [paʊnd] loses its glide it becomes [pand], or *pond*. If *life* [laɪf] loses its glide it becomes [laf], which will be interpreted as *laugh* in New England, parts of Virginia, and perhaps elsewhere as well.

In Southern coastal speech some modification of the above statements must be made. In the South, [ɔl] frequently indicates either *all* or *oil*; [fɔl], both *fall* and *foil*; the context indicates the intended meaning. The reduction of [aɪ] to [a], on the other hand, produces little ambiguity in the South, since [laf] indicates *life* and [læf] indicates *laugh*. In most Southern speech [a] is used only as a variant of [aɪ] and has no other function. Only in Virginia may it require context to interpret [laf] as *life* or *laugh*.

The three phonemic diphthongs, moreover, vary considerably in the shadings with which they are produced. This variability need not trouble the foreigner, who should aim at the principal forms suggested by the symbols [aɪ], [ɔɪ], and [aʊ]. For the native speaker, however, some comment on the variations seems desirable.

The action for [aɪ] consists essentially of a raising of the tongue in the front part of the mouth. If the rise starts too far back, and the diphthong becomes [ɑɪ], it may sound "wrong" to some listeners. If it shifts much further toward [ɔɪ], it will be considered both wrong and ambiguous. This shift is frequently noticeable in the New York City area.

For [ɔɪ] the action consists of a shift from the low-back-tense-rounded [ɔ] to the high-front-lax-unrounded [ɪ]. In Pennsylvania and westward through the Midland area, [ɔɪ] often changes to [oɪ], and the listener rarely notices the change. In New York City a substitution of [ɜɪ] for both [ɔɪ] and [ɜ] produces the so-called "thoity-thoid street accent." Although this shift is no longer as frequent as it used to be, many New Yorkers, including some who use it themselves, regard it with distaste. The Southern coastal area often uses [ɜɪ] for [ɜ], but not for [ɔɪ]. The Southern attitude toward [ɜɪ] is less hostile than the New Yorker's; many Southerners take it for granted. An old-fashioned pronunciation of [aɪ] for [ɔɪ], as in [baɪl] for *boil* and [paɪzən] for *poison,* is now largely confined to isolated rural areas. Only [haɪst] for *hoist* and [raɪl] for *roil* can be heard with any frequency.

The diphthong [ɑʊ] involves a raising of the tongue in the back of the mouth. If the beginning of the rise is further forward, in the form [aʊ], the difference is not likely to be noticed by many listeners. Indeed [aʊ] is frequent from New York City down through the Midland and Southern areas. If, however, the diphthong shifts as far as [æʊ], and *out* begins like *at,* the sensibilities of a good many listeners may be offended.

A special variation is the use of [ɜʊ] when the diphthong precedes a voiceless consonant, as in [ɜʊt] for *out* and [hɜʊs] for *house.* This is a survival from earlier usage which still has status in the Virginia Tidewater, along the Canadian border, and in Canada itself. Although it may sound odd to strangers, [ɜʊ] is a completely normal form in the areas indicated.

The following exercises are designed to give the student practice in acquiring habitual control of the most usual forms of the diphthongs [aɪ], [aʊ], and [ɔɪ].

To avoid [ɑɪ], contrast [aɪ] with [ɑ], and make the beginning of the diphthong more like [æ] :

344: [ɑ] contrasted with [aɪ]

[ɑ]	[aɪ]	[ɑ]	[aɪ]
hah-hah-hah	high	hot-hot-hot	height
mah-mah-mah	my	cot-cot-cot	kite
don-don-don	dine	tahm-tahm-tahm	time
lahf-lahf-lahf	life	far-far-far	fire
fahl-fahl-fahl	file	rod-rod-rod	ride
lock-lock-lock	like	nahs-nahs-nahs	nice

345: Make the beginning of [aɪ] more like [æ]

[æ]	[aɪ]	[æ]	[aɪ]
rap-rap-rap	ripe	tam-tam-tam	pile
hat-hat-hat	height	had-had-had	time
man-man-man	mine	pal-pal-pal	hide
mass-mass-mass	mice	lack-lack-lack	like

346: Contrast [e] and [aɪ]

[e]	[aɪ]	[e]	[aɪ]
may	my	pay	pie
say	sigh	claim	climb
tame	time	waves	wives
main	mine	mate	might
waif	wife	fail	file
race	rice	lake	like

347: Contrast [ɔɪ] and [aɪ]

[ɔɪ]	[aɪ]	[ɔɪ]	[aɪ]
oil	aisle	boy	buy
point	pint	loin	line
foil	file	toil	tile
voice	vice	poise	pies

348: [aɪ]

ice, item, idle, iron, island, fry, fly, thigh, lie, sigh, spy, sky, shy, why, high, pipe, bribe, rhyme, fright, knife, strive, slide, wild, kind, shine, mile, twice, wise, fire, spike, hire.

349: [aɪ] sentences

Try to find the child by five o'clock.
The tired miner lighted his briar pipe.
He spied the writer inside the dining car.
I'll be on the island any time you require.
On a quiet night in July he watched the sky.
Find a common divisor for ninety-nine and fifty-five.

To avoid [æʊ], contrast [æ] with [ɑʊ], pull your tongue back to make the beginning of [ɑʊ] more like [ɑ].

350: [æ] contrasted with [ɑʊ]

[æ]	[ɑʊ]	[æ]	[ɑʊ]
at-at-at	out	pat-pat-pat	pout
lad-lad-lad	loud	clad-clad-clad	cloud
tan-tan-tan	town	hand-hand-hand	hound
lass-lass-lass	louse	trance-trance	trounce

351: Make [ɑʊ] similar at the beginning to [ɑ]

[ɑ]	[ɑʊ]	[ɑ]	[ɑʊ]
aht-aht-aht	out	pot-pot-pot	pout
lahd-lahd-lahd	loud	clod-clod-clod	cloud
tahn-tahn-tahn	town	hahnd-hahnd-hahnd	hound
lahss-lahss-lahss	louse	trahnce-trahnce	trounce

352: Begin [ɑʊ] more like [ɑ]

[ɑ]	[ɑʊ]	[ɑ]	[ɑʊ]
are	hour	pot	pout
trot	trout	shot	shout
prod	proud	clod	cloud
pond	pound	bond	bound

353: Contrast [o] and [ɑʊ]

[o]	[ɑʊ]	[o]	[ɑʊ]
know	now	hoe	how
wrote	rout	float	flout
poach	pouch	coach	couch
load	loud	moaned	mound
tone	town	drone	drown
hole	howl	rose	rouse

354: [aʊ]

out, ounce, owl, bough, cow, scow, how, mouth, south, doubt, stout, crouch, count, mountain, proud, pound, brown, towel, power, browse, houses, lounge, bounce, announce.

355: [aʊ] sentences

The hound sniffed around the hen house.
He counted the cows down in the meadow.
The flowers turned brown in the drought.
The carousing sailors shouted for hours.
The owl flew from the tower to the bough.
He drove a high-powered car through the mountains.

356: [ɔ] and [ɔɪ]

[ɔ]	[ɔɪ]	[ɔ]	[ɔɪ]
all	oil	jaw	joy
saw	soy	cough	coif
lawn	loin	ball	boil
brawl	broil	fall	foil
tall	toil	call	coil
pause	poise	gnaws	noise

To contrast [ɔɪ] with [ɝ], practice Exercise 339, but change the order from [ɔɪ]-[ɝ] to [ɝ]-[ɔɪ]. To contrast [ɔɪ] with [aɪ], practice Exercise 347, but change the order from [ɔɪ]-[aɪ] to [aɪ]-[ɔɪ].

357: [ɔɪ]

oil, ointment, oyster, boy, joy, employ, annoy, destroy, moist, joist, point, joint, join, coin, loyal, foyer, spoil, choice, poison, noise, annoying, adjoin, boiler, voiceless, coil.

358: [ɔɪ] sentences

The boy foiled the theft of the coins.
The adroit workman hoisted the joists.
The poisonous snake curled up in coils.
Roy put soy sauce on the broiled oysters.
She rejoiced in the quiet of the cloister.
The boiler was in a room adjoining the foyer.

INDEX OF SOUNDS

Phonetic symbols, as used in this book, are in approximate alphabetical order. Numbers refer to exercises which provide practice material for the represented sound.

[a] used by some speakers in *ask, dance, path;* by others in *far, farm;* by others in *not, stop, lock;* not used by all speakers: 307.

[ɑ] used by most speakers in *far, farm, not, stop, lock:* 297-303, 307, 309, 310, 337, 344, 351, 352.

[ɒ] used by some speakers in *lost, cough, broth;* by some in *not, stop, lock;* not used by all speakers: 308, 309.

[æ] *cat, ran, ham;* used by most speakers in *ask, dance, path;* by some in *marry, carrot:* 291-298, 307, 345, 350.

[aɪ] *aisle, right, try:* 344-349.

[aʊ] *out, loud, now:* 350-355.

[b] *bob, rubber:* 1-3, 13-21, 42, 43, 56, 139, 179, 246-247.

[d] *did, rudder:* 27, 50, 59, 67-69, 87-90, 97-101, 105-107, 112, 118-120, 126, 128, 142, 180, 200-202, 242-247, 253, 265.

[dʒ] *judge, age, agile:* 200-211, 213.

[ð] *this, father, smooth:* 67-70, 74, 75, 78-81, 85, 86, 173, 180.

[e], [eɪ] *ache, break, say:* 282, 284-287, 290, 292, 316, 346.

[ɛ] *end, get, said;* used by some speakers in *marry, carrot:* 283, 284, 288-291, 293, 336.

[ɝ], [ɜ] *earn, birth, word, fur:* 333-340, 343.

[ə] unstressed vowel of *about, taken, bacon, circus;* also used by some speakers as unstressed vowel of *beggar, proper, tapir, actor, murmur:* 334, 335, 341-343.

[ɚ] used by most speakers as unstressed vowel of *beggar, proper, tapir, actor, murmur:* 341, 343.

[f] *fife, rough, aphid:* 31-41, 44-46, 54, 71-73, 75, 140, 154-156, 160, 269.

[g] *go, ghost, ragged, vague:* 123, 145, 182, 204, 205, 219-222, 242-257, 260, 266, 268.

133

[h]   *how, who, ahead:* 269-275.

[i], [ɪi] *each, bee, machine:* 276-278, 281, 282, 320.

[ɪ]   *inch, build, myth, queer, dear:* 276, 279-281, 283, 293, 335.

[j]   *young, onion, use:* 212-218, 274, 275, 327-332.

[k]   *cat, kick, liquid:* 59, 60, 122, 144, 170, 171, 194, 195, 219-241, 261, 262, 266, 268, 270.

[l]   *let, tall, field:* 2, 5, 7, 14, 32, 37, 87, 115-131, 134-136, 155, 160, 166, 167, 181, 220, 250.

[m]   *maim, summer, limb:* 19-30, 102-104, 168, 179, 232, 259.

[n]   *none, dinner, sign:* 87, 102-117, 169, 181, 232, 258, 259.

[ŋ]   *long, length, anxiety:* 182, 232, 239, 256-268.

[o], [ou] *own, boat, so, crow:* 314-319, 353.

[ɔ]   used by most speakers in *all, law, north, brought;* by some in *lost, cough, broth:* 302-306, 308, 309, 311, 315, 334, 356.

[ɔi] *oil, coin, boy:* 339, 347, 356-358.

[p]   *pop, copper:* 1-12, 25, 31-34, 138, 160, 161, 228-232.

[r]   *red, through, very, carry;* also used by most speakers in *far, farm:* 2, 8, 9, 15, 32, 36, 92, 93, 132-149, 160, 163, 186, 220, 225, 230, 234, 243, 249, 299, 302, 304, 333-337.

[s]   *see, ace, lesson, waltz:* 6, 7, 9, 23, 39, 60, 76, 77, 81, 93, 109, 111, 124, 127, 138, 141, 144, 150-172, 176, 191, 224, 225, 229, 234, 237-239, 262.

[ʃ]   *she, sure, cash, pressure, nation:* 143, 152, 153, 185-189, 192, 193.

[t]   *taught, utter, looked:* 39, 59, 64-66, 87-96, 111, 126, 127, 141, 163-165, 190, 191, 223-232, 238, 239, 262.

[tʃ] *chew, each, nature:* 190-199, 206, 207.

[θ]   *thin, path, ether:* 64-66, 70-73, 75-77, 80-84, 140, 150, 151.

[u], [uu] *ooze, through, moon, rude:* 217, 319, 320, 323, 324, 326-328, 330, 332.

[ʊ]   *put, wolf, should, wood, poor:* 321-323, 325, 326, 329, 330, 332, 335.

[ʌ]   *up, rough, does, flood:* 310-314, 321, 338.

[v]   *valve, oven, Stephen:* 42-53, 56, 57, 74, 75, 174, 179.

[w]   *west, quest;* also used by some speakers in *when, why, somewhat:* 53, 55-61, 63, 92, 132, 133, 136, 162, 170, 273-275.

[ʍ] used by some speakers in *when, why, somewhat:* 54, 55, 57, 62, 63, 271, 273-275.

[z] *zone, gaze, dizzy, rose:* 26, 49, 78, 79, 81, 112, 173-184, 202, 252, 265.

[ʒ] *azure, measure;* used by some speakers in *rouge, bijou:* 175, 185, 188, 189, 203.